HEADCASE

A True Story of Love, Life, Medical Miracles & Battling Against the Odds

John Walsh

This edition printed and bound in the Republic of Ireland by:

Clódóirí CL Printing
Unit 7 Costelloe Industrial Estate,
Casla, Co. Galway.

Co-authored by Kathryn Rogers.

ISBN: 978-1-5262-0547-6.

For Edel, Fírinne, Ríain, and Saorla, my reasons to never give up.

Acknowledgements

I've dedicated this book to my wife, Edel, love of my life, best friend and the one who is always by my side and always has my back. It's also dedicated to my beloved children, Fírinne, Ríain, and Saorla, who give me the determination to fight and who have the ability to make me laugh and cry – often at the same time!

There are also a lot of other people who have contributed in many different ways to this book especially my mother, Carmel, and my late father, Patrick, who've done so much for me. My mother is always there when the chips are down. Thanks, Mam.

Thanks too to my twin, Cathy, and siblings, Linda, Laura, Alma, and Padraic who are always there for me. And to my brothers-in-law, Fergal and Andrew, and future sister-in-law, Laura G, for providing even more back up.

Also, Edel's extended family, the Tobins and Ryans, for their ongoing support and making me feel like one of the Tipperary mafia!

My aunt, uncles and all the Winston, Walsh and Kelly cousins for the numerous ways that they've supported me.

There are so many in the medical profession who I need to thank for their significant roles in my care down through the years. Foremost among them is the doctor who knows my medical file like no other, Professor Frank Sullivan. Over the years, Frank has become someone that I infinitely trust. I want to thank him wholeheartedly for everything he's done since we first met in 2005.

Also, I need to send special thanks to the staff in the radiation department of University Hospital Galway. I'm one of the longest attending patients, and I was there within hours of getting married and having my first child so, I've shared many significant milestones with the incredible team there.

Thanks especially to the wonderful Dr Anna Marie O Connell, my radiologist in University Hospital Galway for all her help over the years and for reducing the stress of waiting for scan results! Also thanks, Anna Marie, for having the patience to answer all my many questions.

Other life savers include Dr Claire Faul, for overseeing my most recent CyberKnife treatment and for guiding me on my treatment options. Also Dr David Allcutt for taking on my file and treatment when I returned from Germany in 2001 and Dr David O Brien who has managed to keep me intact despite several high-risk surgeries on my spine!

To Dr Maccon Keane, Oncologist in University Hospital Galway, and Dr Patrick Morris Oncologist in Beaumont Hospital for overseeing my chemo treatment and always being kind and generous with their help and opinions; To Dr Jamsari Khalid and Dr Nazir Ibrahim, my great radiation consultants in Dublin and Galway.

To Catherine Brady Copertino, who navigated my path to a second opinion at Memorial Sloan Kettering Cancer Centre, New York, one of the top research hospitals in the world. To Dr Thomas Kaley at Memorial Sloan Kettering for all his help and reassurance. Thanks too to Dr Patrick Boland, a fellow Irishman, for being so generous with his time and advice from the U.S.

Thanks to my GP in 2010, Susan Kennelly and all staff at Adrian Carney's, Roscam Medical Centre. Also to Dr Declan Egan and Dr Una Conway and all the staff at Galway Fertility Clinic.

There are too many kind and amazing staff to thank individually for my care and treatment in Zentralkrankanhaus Hospital, Bremen; Memorial Sloan Kettering Hospital New York; University Hospital Galway; Beaumont Hospital in Dublin, and the radiation department of The Hermitage Clinic in Dublin.

I'd also like to extend thanks and appreciation to Mike Carty and Annie Gaynor in New York, Joe Fenton in Boston and the other people who helped me in the U.S.A.

There are lots of other remarkable people that I want to thank especially my amazing colleagues and friends at Tusla for all the support they give. They are too numerous to list, but you know who you are! Also thanks to the staff of the HSE organisation where I used to work. Special thanks to Ross Cullen, my good friend and communications guru, and to Olivia Collins, Marilyn Reddan and Cathy Curran for all their help with the PR as well.

Thanks, as ever, to all staff and fellow patients at Cancer Care West Galway for ongoing support of my family and me and the wonderful, Helen Greally for her encouragement and teaching me the skills to mentally cope.

To Detail.ie for doing such a fantastic job on my book cover. I may have to retrace my steps many times in this life and be forced to follow another route, but in the end, I hope to get there!

Thanks to C.L. Printing's Michael, Gearoid, Tom and Conall. Also to Keith Finnegan, Ollie Turner and all at Galway Bay FM; to the very special Mary McGuire for saying at least one holy hour for me every week since 2000; to John O'Connor for transporting me to Beaumont Hospital in the early days; to all our good neighbours and friends, for the friendly text, call, card, babysitting or hot dinners when needed.

Thanks to the extended staff and parents at Naomi's Crèche, Knocknacarra, for taking such amazing care of our children no matter what the hour, to Lorna Siggins for pointing me in the right direction to complete my dream of writing a book, to literary agent Jonathan Williams for his help, the lovely Orla Kelly of orlakellypublishing.com for helping publish my book online and to Micháel Reidy for all his help and advice especially with the photography. Thanks to our parish priest, Fr Gerry Jennings for the use of Pope Francis's 10 Tips for Happiness and all his support over the years.

Thanks too to Louis Walsh, and Padraic Joyce, my schoolmate and friend, for their support.

A very special thanks and appreciation to John Lonergan for all his advice, and help, and for agreeing to launch this book.

CONTENTS

No matter how you feel,
get up, dress up, show up,
and never give up.

Anon.

PROLOGUE

My body feels far too heavy; I gasp for breath with every step. The pain in my head is unbearable and waves of nausea roll over me.

Resting a sweat-slicked forehead on the door, I fumble with the key in the lock. Home at last. Music beats in my flatmate David's room and I'm relieved that I'm not alone.

It feels safer to leave the bedroom door open, so I keep it ajar by kicking the laundry in its way.

It's a steamy July evening, but I shiver in a film of cold sweat. Peeling off damp clothes feels like a Herculean task. I stop twice to get my breath before stripping down to boxer shorts. Sinking onto the creaking bed, I'd like to lie down, but I'm too nauseous, too breathless.

The room spins. The left side of my face is cold and numb, and my left arm is heavy. My heart hammers in my rib cage. It's hard to breathe, but I know I have to wait. This will pass like it did before. Relax. The doctor says it's anxiety. It's a panic attack. Nothing to worry about.

Yet, deep down, I know he's wrong. I hear a clock that no one else hears, and it's counting down. I want to believe it's nothing but all I feel is doom. I wait and wait but now my tongue feels strange. It grows bigger;

moves of its own accord. Stop imagining things. Stay calm. Still, it swells; fills my mouth and slowly, very slowly it curls back into my throat.

I can't stop it; can't control it. I gag and choke and try to fight, but I'm swallowing my tongue. Is that even possible?

I can't breathe. I jab fingers in my mouth, but my tongue is lodged back in my throat. It blocks my airways. I scream inside my head, but a strange gurgling is the only sound in the room. This can't be it. I don't want to die like this.

My heart beats faster; adrenalin courses through me, and now it's clear what I need to do. I scramble a few steps to the kitchen, rifle in the drawer for a soup spoon and try to force it in my mouth.

Somewhere, somehow I remember this is what you do to stop someone choking on their tongue. I wrestle the tongue that's choking me, try press it back to the floor of my mouth, and try to make a gap for air. The adrenaline ebbs away and so does my strength. My legs slide away from under me, and I slip down the wall to the floor...

David's familiar face is among several strange ones looming over me. His face is a mask of fear. I gasp like a landed fish on the linoleum floor, still gripping the spoon in my mouth. Trembling and terrified, yet relieved I can almost breathe again.

A blonde girl my own age kneels by me, smiling and stroking my hand. Other faces above jostle for position. A man in a paramedic's uniform crouches in front of me. He's coaxing me to release the spoon from my mouth.

David's pleading with people to tell him what's wrong with me, but he's speaking in English. Everyone else is speaking in German. I can't speak at all.

The paramedic has a brown paper bag. He signals that he wants me to breathe into it. He assumes that like David, I don't speak German either.

"Mit ihm ist nichts falsch," he reassures the crowded room. "Es ist alles in seinem kopf."

But I understand perfectly, and if I could breathe properly, I'd cry with despair.

"There's nothing wrong with him," he says. "It's all in his head."

It turns out he was right in a way.

AUF WIEDERSEHEN

After dashing through the airport with my case clattering behind me, I rushed to the boarding gate with a broad smile across my face.

The woman behind the desk fixed my beaming face with a stony stare before glancing at my ticket and passport. I couldn't have cared less. Not even a thunder-faced airline attendant could dampen the sense of exhilaration I felt that day.

Scanning the sea of faces on the plane, I spotted the one I knew. I slammed my case into a gap in the overhead bin and slumped heavily into the seat beside David Lynch.

"Can you believe this is happening?" I said, elbowing him in the ribs. "We must be the luckiest guys ever. A new country, new jobs, new life, loadsamoney!"

Grinning back, he injected a small note of caution into our new adventure.

"Let's not get too excited, will we? Let's see what the city of Bremen is like and what British Airways is like to work for first!"

"Oh, come on!" I argued. "Whatever it's like, it's got to be better than exams and studying and being flat broke all the time!"

As far as I was concerned, working for Deutsche British Airways was a dream job. A blue chip international company with decent pay and conditions, I couldn't have imagined a better start to my career.

Heading for their head-office and the brighter lights of Bremen, I was 23 years old and couldn't have been happier.

Dad forlornly waved me off at Dublin Airport that Saturday morning, April 29th, 2000. Minutes later, I'd already cast my life in rural Liskeavy, Co. Galway to the furthest recesses of my mind.

Brimming with confidence, I was convinced this job was the opportunity to change my world forever. I felt invincible, assured and on top of the world. I was a completely different to the man I am today.

Back then I could never have guessed the dramatic and unforeseen ways that my fate was about to twist. I certainly couldn't have conceived that within weeks, my life would be hanging by a thread and that the course of my future was about to shift forever.

Instead, that day my head was just fizzing with the thrill of travel and the prospect of a new life.

"What are we going to spend all that money on?" I mused. "4,000 Deutschmarks is two grand a month. I might just go mad. I won't know myself with money."

"Don't start buying race cars until we get a roof over our heads," said David. "We've only got a month before we have to find a place to live."

I was convinced that the Deutsche B.A. recruiters were very smart to have spotted my singular brilliance. I was one of the hundreds who sweated through a series of exams in overheated rooms in Jury's Hotel in Dublin.

My test scores were just above average, so I might have been written out of the application process at that stage. Thankfully, I still got to the interview and as soon as I showcased my flawless German language skills, one of the five jobs on offer with Deutsche B.A. was mine.

German came easily to me even though I was a lazy student. By the time I was in my teens and on a school exchange to Bavaria, I spoke it as fluently as English.

I was just completing a two-year diploma course in German and IT studies in Galway when the interviews for these jobs in Bremen arose.

Travelling to a strange city, meeting different people and starting a new job were all exhilarating to me.

"Let's hope there are loads of pubs and clubs there," I said. "I want to try all the German dance clubs. Maybe when we get our place, we can have lots of parties and meet loads of girls! I wonder if there are any sports clubs we could join?"

David raised an eyebrow.

"Yeah, I'm sure we can join the local hurling team in Bremen," he snorted. "There's probably a G.A.A. Club on every corner. I don't know if you'll have the time, though. Won't you be too busy beating all those German women off you with a stick?"

"That's also true!" I said with a laugh.

I never cared if anyone thought I was cocky in those days because I felt I had a right to be. I figured I was great. On top of everything, the new job offered not only a new life in Germany, but also a chance to see the world.

"You know we're going to be able to go anywhere we want?" I said. "We can buy plane tickets to anywhere in the world now for 10% of the regular fare."

"You know we don't get that staff perk for months?" he said. "You could be out of the job by then."

Not in my head. I was hugely ambitious and believed I was destined for far greater things.

"Speak for yourself. They'll probably dump you all right, but they're going to love me. I'm going to be president of Deutsche B.A. one day. Wait and see!"

We were among five young Irish recruits who flew out from Dublin airport that weekend.

David, from Mayo, was hired to join Deutsche's French language team. We knew each other from college and even though he was quieter in nature than me, we shared a common interest in GAA, music and girls.

"What are you going to do when you get to Bremen? You don't speak a word of German," I laughed.

"I don't need to worry, do I?" he replied. "You talk enough for the both of us."

A company representative collected us on arrival and delivered us to a featureless airport hotel that was our home for the next month. We had free accommodation there for the first few weeks of induction training.

The training began two days later. We arrived at Deutsche BA's corporate offices on Monday, May 1 and we looked up awestruck at the ultra-modern facade. The building, with its giant panels of glass and steel, glittered coldly in the morning sun. It was like something I'd only seen on T.V. before.

Once inside the building, even the flooring underfoot gleamed white. It was all so vast and futuristic; it made me even more impressed with our new jobs.

"Jesus, David, it's like being in a sci-fi movie," I said. "It's like we're on the set of Mission Impossible here."

It was an instant love affair for me. I loved being part of this shiny Vorsprung Durch Technik world where anything seemed possible.

One of seven staff on the German-Irish team, I worked the night shift from 7.00pm to 6.00am. The job involved handling administration and dealing with customer calls around a big desk on an enormous open plan floor. It was busy, buzzy and hectic and the kind of environment I thrived in.

I didn't mind working the night shift. It suited me to sleep half the day and to work all night. There was something magical about working at night and watching the city twinkle all around us. From our big picture windows, we could see the bright strobe lights of the planes approaching and landing at the airport nearby.

Within days of arriving, my new line manager slapped a pile of documents in front of me.

"Sign these. Head office is waiting for them," he said.

They were forms for our new health insurance policy, which required a contribution from the employees.

"I've never been sick a day in my life," I said. "I could do without any extra expenses at the moment. Can I join later?"

Hermann, the line manager, raised his eyes in exasperation. He didn't understand these cheeky young foreigners who dared to question company policy.

"Sign the papers!" he barked. "Medical insurance is not an optional extra. It's the law! "

As our free hotel accommodation came to an end, David and I realised it was time to find a permanent place to live. I spotted an ad for a suitable apartment in the city's accommodation magazine.

"This one is about seven stops away on the S-Bahn," I said jabbing a finger at a page of the magazine. "We can afford it, and the ad says it's 'mobiliert'. It's furnished."

Neither of us fancied shopping for furniture and kitchenware, so I rang the listed number and got an address so we could view the place. The address brought us to a three storey, stone-fronted house in a leafy suburb of Bremen.

The landlady, Hildegarde Fuhrmann, opened her door and cast a suspicious eye over the two young Irishmen there. Her blonde-grey hair was swept up in a traditional crown of braids, and she was tall and formidable despite being in her eighties.

"Your references, please!" she said extending a demanding palm towards us. She appeared reluctant to let us in, but she relented and led us through her house to the flat.

"I occupy these two floors of the property," she announced. "The apartment for rent is at the top of the stairs."

Plush carpets muted our footsteps on the stairs. We glanced up at glittering chandeliers and carefully skirted around the elegant antique furnishings. We caught glimpses of gilt-framed old artworks on the walls as we followed her to the second floor flat.

The splendour of Hildegarde's accommodation was in stark contrast to the spartan flat above. The apartment for rent contained two small bedrooms each

11

furnished with a bed, lino floors and walls painted a neutral shade of sludge.

The highlight of the flat's galley kitchen was a hob with two electric rings. The place seemed as joyless and grim as the landlady watching us.

"It's clean, and it has beds and stuff," I whispered to David.

He didn't seem too convinced.

"I know she seems like a bit of a battle axe, but we don't have to stay for long," I urged. "This will do for six months until we save a bit of money and we can move on to something better."

We told Frau Fuhrmann that we'd like to rent the apartment but her lips puckered with resistance.

"I'll take your name and number, and I'll think about it," she said. "I don't know if you're suitable for my apartment. I've never had two single men as tenants. I keep a spotless house."

"Really Frau Fuhrmann, we're very tidy," I assured her in my fluent German. "We work all night, and we'll be sleeping most of the day so you won't even know we're here. You can also see our references from the company. We have secure jobs so you'll never have a problem getting the rent."

Hildegarde couldn't resist the cash deposit in our hands so, within days, we moved into our humble new home.

As we carried our belongings up the stairs into our new accommodation, I passed a black and white photo of a man in full Nazi uniform standing behind prison bars. Curiosity got the better of me.

"If you don't mind me asking, who is the man in the photo, Frau Fuhrmann?"

"That is my father. He was an S.S. Officer, a wonderful man," she said with glistening eyes.

She indicated the walls crammed with old oil paintings.

"He loved art - he accumulated all this artwork during the war," she explained.

Later, she showed us a cherished album filled with sepia-toned photos of her father posing with the infamous leaders of the Third Reich.

We soon discovered our new landlady ran her household with the same intimidation tactics as the Third Reich. She liked to mount blitzkrieg inspections of our apartment and would fly into a fury if she found grease in the pan, a dish in the sink or an unmade bed.

"I will not stand for any untidiness or filth in my house!" she harrumphed after each incursion.

She was never without her trusty dust cloth. Anytime we saw her she was vigorously polishing and cleaning her palatial surroundings.

Then one day we got in from work and found her fluffy white Persian pawing something around the stairs.

"What's that cat got?" said David trying to see what the feline was now possessively guarding. He recoiled.

"Jesus, I think it's a dead rat!"

"You're kidding me!"

"Well, it's a dead mouse anyway!"

We shook with smothered laughter as I wrestled the kill from the cat and picked up the rodent by the tip of its tail.

"Oh, Frau Fuhrmann!" I yelled. "Can we see you for a moment?"

Hildegarde bustled out of her kitchen with customary speed. She was probably about to attack us over another cleaning infraction.

Instead, I wiggled the evidence of vermin in her spotless fortress.

Her face reddened, and her eyes bulged.

"Frau Fuhrmann, we're just wondering, does this belong to you?" I asked trying to keep a straight face.

She glowered at us as she snatched the mouse and stomped back to her kitchen without a word.

We stumbled up the stairs convulsing with laughter.

It was a small victory in the war with Hildegarde so it was a good day. It was one of the last good days I remember having in Germany.

ACHTUNG DOCTOR!

Just weeks after we'd moved into Hildegarde's apartment, I started to feel unwell. It began on a fine morning in June after I'd finished a shift at work. A German colleague dropped me home and, after waving him off, I was hit by a crashing headache and a wave of nausea.

By the time I got up the two flights of stairs and into our apartment, the pain was excruciating. It was like something savage had stuck its fangs through the top of my head and was sucking out the contents. My skull felt as if it was being crushed and my cheekbones being dragged up to meet my eyes.

Then suddenly I couldn't breathe. Something had turned off all the air.

As I shook in silent terror, I saw strange red pulses of blood shooting through a vein in my index finger. I wondered was I going mad. I thought I was about to pass out; I'd never experienced anything like it before.

Then in less than 30 seconds, it stopped as abruptly as it began.

I sat trembling for ages afterwards. Whatever had happened was brief but it frightened me enough to make an appointment with a doctor that day.

I found the GP's surgery on the ground floor of a modern apartment block on a manicured, residential street of Bremen. Dr Wolfgang Voertig-Hoffmann was a distinguished-looking man in his 50s with steel-rimmed spectacles. He leant forward on his desk and considered me carefully behind a steeple of fingers.

"Do you think you could be homesick or anxious?" he asked. "It sounds like you had a panic attack or perhaps, an asthma attack."

I was sceptical.

"I don't miss home, and I don't think it was a panic attack," I replied. "I've never had asthma before in my life. I don't think I ever felt anxious before either, but I do now."

"It seems you have had a panic attack," he said. "The symptoms you experienced seem very real, and it's very frightening, but it's also very common. I'm going to prescribe some anti-anxiety medication for you. You're going to be fine."

I was happy to accept his assurances. After all, I felt ridiculous being in a doctor's surgery. Of course, I was fine; I was a healthy 23-year-old for God's sake. I'd rarely been inside a doctor's surgery and had never been in hospital in my life.

In fact, a diagnosis of a panic attack came as a relief because I wanted to believe that there was nothing physically the matter with me.

"Maybe I am stressed being in a new country but I just didn't realise it," I said.

The relief I got in the doctor's surgery didn't last long though because, within days, I was sick again. This time, the thundering headaches came in waves that lasted hours at a time.

"Did you try an Aspirin or a paracetamol?" asked David.

"I've tried everything. I was up half the night with headaches, and feeling sick" I said. "I'm exhausted from lack of sleep. I just don't know what to do."

I couldn't even tell him about the eerie silence I started noticing in my head too. It was too difficult to explain, and he might think I was mad. This silence was so loud that it seemed like it was taking over my head. I began to wonder if, perhaps, I really was going mad.

One night at work, I looked so ashen that an older German colleague called Anja Baumann urged me to go to the hospital.

"I think you're right," I said. "My doctor isn't listening to me. I'll go to the hospital after my shift is finished. "

She directed me to the Zentralkrankenhaus (Central Hospital) in Bremen by train. I expected a long wait, but there was a world of difference between this hospital and the overcrowded A&E departments back home. After taking a seat in an almost vacant waiting room, I was seen within minutes.

"What exactly are the symptoms that you're experiencing and what medications are you on?" the A&E doctor asked.

I listed off my afflictions and told him that my doctor had only prescribed me with anti-anxiety medication.

The doctor took me behind a curtain and tested my reflexes by tapping my knee with a rubber hammer. He looked into the back of my eyes and checked for weakness in the muscles of my face, eyes and tongue. He ordered me to follow some simple commands like to close my eyes and touch my nose. Then he gave me a clean bill of health and told me to go home.

"You seem like a perfectly well, young man," he said. "There's nothing serious going on. Take an aspirin for your headache and you'll be fine."

"I've taken aspirins, I've taken everything," I said. "I'm like this for weeks now."

The doctor was dismissive.

"You need to give the anti-anxiety medicine time to work. Stop worrying; you'll be fine."

He might as well have accused me of inventing or imagining my symptoms. I held my aching head in my hands on the way home on the train. I felt hopeless and wretched. I didn't know who to turn to next.

As the week wore on, the headaches and nausea escalated, and I felt progressively worse.

My eyes had trouble focusing, and I felt lightheaded, but I was weighed down by exhaustion. Then days after that hospital visit, I experienced the most terrifying episode of all.

It was hot, humid July evening and yet my skin prickled with beads of cold sweat. I felt I might throw up everywhere so I asked to leave work early. My line manager Hermann raised his eyes. I felt miserable enough, but it made me feel worse when my colleagues thought I was skiving off work.

I hardly made it to the front door of the apartment. I was lathered in a cold sweat by now despite the oppressive heat and a struggle up two flights of stairs. This time, the headache had a savage intensity. My skull felt it was being crushed in a steel vice. The left side of my face and my left arm were numb.

I stripped off my sweat soaked clothes in my room and slumped onto the bed. I sat panting, trying to cope with the searing pain in my head when I began feeling the strangest sensation. My tongue was growing bigger and bigger in my mouth.

No, I thought, I must be imagining it. It seemed to be filling my mouth and curling back of its own accord. It happened so fast, and suddenly I couldn't breathe at all.

My airways were obstructed, and I couldn't make a sound. I was suffocating silently. Somewhere in my mind, I realised that a faint gurgling in the room was me.

My heart banged in terror. I felt trapped in a waking nightmare. I thought that I had seconds to live.

Somewhere, some old wives' tale about using a spoon to stop someone choking on their tongue flashed in my mind. It was all I could think of to do. Staggering to the kitchen, I grabbed a spoon, forced it into my mouth and tried to free my airways.

David found me lying in the kitchen, barely conscious with a spoon in my mouth; my face was mottled black from lack of oxygen.

"Oh, God, hold on John, hold on!" he cried. "I'm calling an ambulance. I'll be right back just hold on! "

Neither of us had bought mobile phones in Germany so he made a panicked dash downstairs to use Hildegarde's house phone. She was away that weekend and he discovered that she had unplugged the phone and locked it away in case we might use it.

He ran out onto the street in desperation.

"Please, please someone help me!" he pleaded. "Someone call an ambulance! It's an emergency!"

He had no German and most people in the north-western city of Bremen didn't speak English. Nevertheless, a few Good Samaritans followed the frenzied looking man up the stairs, and once they saw me on the floor, they called an ambulance.

By the time the paramedics arrived, the worst of the symptoms had receded. I was petrified, but at least I could nearly breathe again. The paramedics indicated for me to breathe into a brown paper bag. They thought I was like David and I didn't speak German.

"Mit ihm ist nichts falsch," said one of the paramedics to everyone around him. "Es ist alles in seinem kopf."

"There's nothing wrong with him," he said. "It's all in his head."

Then they packed up and left. David and I gazed at each other in shock and terror. He was pale-faced and as traumatised as I was. He raged at the dismissive response of the paramedics.

"I just don't understand - why won't anyone just listen to you?" he said. "Jesus, I couldn't believe the colour of you. I was convinced that you were going to die on me! Why won't they do something?"

I felt sure I was going to die too. I knew I had almost choked to death that night. I heard a clock start to tick over my head, and it was ticking down. Call it intuition, sixth sense or anything you want; I felt like I didn't have a lot of time. I just couldn't figure out what to do about it.

I knew that this thing, whatever it was, was going to kill me if I didn't get it first.

HEADCASE

In the days after the paramedics left, I was so sick that I either had to keep leaving work early or else I couldn't go in at all.

"Honestly Hermann, I feel so bad that I can't work; I need to go home," I pleaded.

It was frustrating because I knew my German supervisor suspected I was slacking. It didn't help that the doctors insisted that I was only suffering from panic attacks.

By now I had become friendlier with my co-worker, Anja. On a few occasions when I felt well, we met in the canteen for lunch or we chatted in the corridors. She was one of the few Germans that I'd met there who had perfect English. Anja was a short and stocky woman in her forties with sympathetic sloe-eyes.

"I'm very concerned about you," she said. "I can see by your colour that you're not well. You have to go back to your doctor and get help."

I rang the surgery, but the doctor's schedule was full for the week. The earliest appointment I could get with him was the Monday of the following week. Meanwhile, I got a call from my mother to tell me my maternal granddad, Austin Winston, had died. He had been ill for a long time after suffering a bad stroke seven years earlier.

"I'm sorry to hear that Mam," I said. "I hope you'll be OK. Don't worry; I'll be back in time for his funeral."

By now I felt so tired that just walking felt like wading neck-deep through treacle. I was suffering from double vision and stabbing headaches. The pressure on the plane may not have helped because the pain in my head was so intense that I began to doubt I'd live to make my doctor's appointment on Monday.

To this day, the most vivid memory of the funeral is staring at my granddad's open grave and wondering how long it would be before they buried me beside him.

I didn't say anything to my mother because I could see she had enough to worry about with her father's death. And I didn't want to say anything to anyone else, in case they made me go to the local hospital. I wanted to get back to Germany, see my doctor and keep my job.

I tried to focus on my appointment with my GP after the weekend. This time, I would be firm and insist that he do some proper tests.

My father drove me back to the airport that Sunday. I felt so bad that I hardly said a word to him during the three-hour journey to Dublin.

"I don't know what it is, but there's something seriously wrong with that fella," he told my mother when he got back to Galway that day.

But Dr Voertig-Hoffman didn't believe that there was anything seriously wrong when I returned to his surgery the next day. Instead, he now insisted the stress

23

of my grandfather's death was adding to my anxiety and the escalation in symptoms.

"Don't worry, it's perfectly normal to feel like this after a shock or bereavement," he said. "You're going to feel really bad especially when you're away from all your family and friends."

There was nothing I could do to persuade the man that I wasn't having stress headaches and panic attacks.

"You're a young man; you need to relax," he said. "Go out and enjoy yourself more and stop worrying."

He prescribed more anti-anxiety pills. I left his surgery feeling sick, disoriented, and completely defeated. I knew I was very ill, but I was clueless about which tests to request. The internet was still in its infancy, and Dr Google wasn't around back then. I just didn't know what to do.

I wasn't well enough to go to work that night or following nights. Even though I was too sick to work, I was too afraid to stay at home alone. Hildegarde was away again, and David was working most of the time.

Terrified that I'd have another attack while on my own, I spent miserable days travelling on the busy S-Bahn. My nights were just as awful. I couldn't sleep with the pain, so I'd sit upright in bed with the light on and willing daylight to come.

During one of my long, unhappy jaunts on the S-Bahn, I saw a church spire and on an impulse, got off the train.

Peering through the open door, it felt cool and peaceful. I went in and knelt at a pew. There was no one around so I put my head in my hands and sobbed from sheer exhaustion and despair. I wasn't there long before a priest interrupted my misery. I'm not sure of the denomination of the church, but he was wearing a traditional black cassock.

"Is there anything I can do to help?" he asked placing a comforting hand on my shoulder.

It was a relief to talk to someone even if the advice was familiar.

"You have to go back to the hospital," he urged. "You were probably just unlucky the first time. I'm sure if you go back to the hospital and see a different doctor, they'll sort you out."

It made sense when he said it, so I set out for the hospital with renewed optimism. A&E didn't have any file from my previous visit so another doctor took the same information again and did the same reflex checks again.

"You have all the symptoms of stress," said the doctor. "Shortness of breath, hyperventilation, nausea, heart palpitations and choking feelings are all signs of a panic attack. You're perfectly healthy. You need to calm down and give your anti-anxiety medications a chance to work."

So within the hour, I was back on the S-Bahn and heading for home. I felt hopeless; no one was listening to me. Convinced that I was about to die, I pulled out an A-5 notepad from work and composed a farewell letter to my mother. I was careful to write down her full name, address and telephone number with the full international prefix, as I didn't know who might find it. Underneath, I scribbled a few lines.

It read: 'Hi Mam, I didn't want to say anything to you at Granddad's funeral, but I haven't been well, and if you get this note, I'm probably dead. I did try to get help, but no one would listen to me in the hospital. I'm sorry for all the trouble I've caused, but I want you to know that I love you and Dad and my sisters and brother."

It was very dramatic, but that's how bad I felt at the time. I had learned a lesson from the night I couldn't breathe, and I owned a mobile phone now in case of another seizure. My colleague, Anja, knew I was going to the hospital again so she rang me during the train journey home.

"So what did the hospital say?"

"They said I'm fine and that I should give my anti-anxiety medications more time to work. I'm on my way home now."

"You can't be serious!"

"Look, I've a really big favour to ask, Anja," I said. "Is there any way you could meet me at the station? I've something important that I want to give to you."

Anja was waiting for me when the train pulled in. I pressed the letter I'd scribbled into her hand.

I was grateful for Anja's attention even if I was starting to worry about her intentions. At first, I saw her as a kindly, motherly type, but lately, I began to suspect her feelings for me were not entirely maternal. I wasn't sure, though.

At times I thought that maybe she was just an affectionate and demonstrative woman. But her frequent hugs, kisses and her desire to hold my hand were starting to worry me.

"Thank you so much for doing this Anja, I need you to get this to my mother if anything happens to me," I said. "I honestly think that I'll be dead by the morning. I feel really ill, and I'm getting worse. I really think I'm dying."

She looked at me stunned, scanned the tragic note that I'd written and then took a deep breath.

"That's it - get into my car!" she said bundling me towards the car park. "We're going back to the hospital, and we're not leaving until we get answers."

We returned to the same hospital but this time, a determined Anja was in control. In A&E, she was loud and insistent and demanded that they do something immediately.

"Do you realise he's so sick that he's no longer at work?" she argued. "We're not leaving here until you do some proper tests and find out what's going on!" There was a murmured discussion among a few nurses and a doctor. They looked over my file, and they looked over at me. They made a few phone calls and had a few more quiet discussions. Then after a half an hour or so, a nurse approached and said she was bringing me to Dr Beckenbauer's office.

As I was led in, the doctor was already sitting at a desk located at the far end of a dark, long room. He motioned for me to sit on a chair positioned just inside the door. It was a good twenty feet away from him, so I felt like a specimen in a jar rather than a patient. The only light in the room was behind him so that I could see little more than his silhouette. I thought it was an odd set up for a doctor's office.

He asked my age, date of birth and then he asked if I had a girlfriend. He quizzed me about friends, home life and everything including what I had for breakfast. This personal interrogation went on for more than twenty minutes. I wondered about the strange line of questioning, but I was happy to cooperate.

It was only the next day that I learned Dr Beckenbauer was the hospital psychiatrist, and my 'consultation' was a psychiatric assessment. Anja learned the truth that night when she stopped a nurse to ask how I was. She was shaken to hear that I was in the middle of a psych evaluation. When she mentioned it to me the next morning, she was furious to learn that I knew nothing about it.

"They are taking advantage of you being a foreigner," she fumed. "That would never happen to a German citizen without their consent and knowledge."

I didn't care. The doctors could have asked me to stand on my head and wear a Donald Duck costume, and I'd have been happy to comply. I was grateful for any medical attention.

I never heard the results of the psych test, but thanks to Anja's dogged persistence the hospital finally agreed to investigate further. However, they made it clear that they thought further medical tests were unnecessary.

"We don't believe there's anything wrong," said a doctor. "But because of your high levels of anxiety, we'll admit you for the night and do some investigations to put your mind at rest."

I let out a huge sigh. I was so relieved that I almost cried. Anja came to the rescue yet again when she volunteered to pack a bag at my apartment and bring it back to the hospital.

Meanwhile, the doctor repeated their usual reflex tests. They insisted the paralysis I felt down the left side of my body was a symptom of my anxiety and hysteria.

Dr Günter Schmidt was now in charge of my case. He was a youngish man in his late thirties or early forties, with a bald head, round glasses and a curt manner.

"The only thing we can do is carry out an MRI brain scan," he said. "We don't have the facility in this hospital but take a look at this list and decide in which of these three hospitals, you want to have the scan?"

The scan, scheduled for 6.00am, couldn't come soon enough. At that stage, the entire left-hand side of my face and left arm had lost all feeling. The numbness was creeping down my left leg now too. Headaches, dizziness, and nausea were my constant companions. I had spots in my eyes and distorted vision. I was terrified of choking again.

Dr Schmidt still didn't believe an MRI was warranted. Either he thought I was a malingerer or just a head case, but he believed that it was all a complete waste of his time and of hospital resources.

"You're perfectly fine, you know," he said. "But the scan will prove that."

The last thing he said as he left the room was: "Have your bags packed afterwards. Your discharge time is 11.00am."

An ambulance transferred me to the MRI imaging centre early in the morning. I don't remember much about it. Instead, I watched the clock and dreaded the approach of 11.00am when I'd have to leave the hospital.

By the time they transferred me back to my room in Zentralkrankenhaus, it must have been around 9.00am. I knew I should get packed and dressed, but I was terrified at the prospect of going home. What was I going to do once I left the hospital?

Dr Schmidt was expressionless when he came to the room shortly before 10.00am. I thought he'd arrived to tell me to leave early.

"Herr Walsh, come to room 26 with me," he said in his usual brusque manner.

The exact number "sechsundzwanzig" is etched forever in my mind. I trailed after him down the hall to a small box-shaped office with a desk, my file and two seats. He indicated that I take one of them.

There was no preamble.

"Herr Walsh, you have a brain tumour," he said. "It is putting pressure on your brain stem. This growth is causing your headaches and breathing problems. I'm afraid we need to operate immediately. We'll be scheduling surgery for tomorrow."

He paused to let the news sink in. I sat stunned for a few seconds, and my eyes began to well up. Then I got unsteadily to my feet and grabbed the startled doctor in a bear hug.

I had a brain tumour! I was over the moon. It was like I won the Lotto.

FRAU ROBINSON

It's called a liponeurocytoma, which is a big name for a small tumour. For weeks, they didn't know what kind of growth it was. The hospital sent it around four different labs in the World Health Organisation before they identified it. It turned out to be an extremely rare form of tumour.

Only 40 cases of liponeurocytoma have been reported in the world since it was first classified in 1978. So I really did win a lotto of sorts.

The day of my surgery, Saturday, July 22nd, 2000, we didn't know any of that. Neither did we know if the growth as benign or malignant.

All they knew for sure was the tumour was located in a precarious spot at the base of my skull beside the brainstem. The brain stem controls everything from breathing to seeing, hearing, walking and talking. It's an area of the brain that you don't want to mess with unless you have to.

Things moved fast after the diagnosis. German efficiency swung into action, and an entire medical team descended to plan for the surgery the next day.

There were more scans, more tests and lots of people in white coats and clipboards swarmed around to prod and poke me.

Anja was there, throughout, holding my hand, hugging me and being far too familiar for my liking. I was 23, and I liked age appropriate relationships. I'd never harboured fantasies of a Mrs Robinson-style relationship. A matronly Mrs Robinson, like Anja, certainly didn't appeal to me at all. Yet, here she was, by my bed, suffocating me with her affections.

"Oh you poor, poor darling, let me hold you," she exclaimed when she first heard I had a brain tumour.

She grasped my face in both her plump hands, fixed her big black-brown eyes on me and planted frenzied kisses on my face.

"I'm fine, Anja, really I'm fine," I said trying to wriggle out of her tenacious grip.

I was a man in pyjamas with a very severe headache trapped by a middle-aged colleague who had abandoned all sense of propriety and personal space. Feeling self-conscious and mortified, I may have only imagined everyone staring at me and my amorous, forty-something companion.

Apart from Anya's unwanted attentions, I was still relieved and happy about my diagnosis. For the first time in a couple of months, I felt I was going to survive this ordeal. The doctors had located the source of my problems at last, and they were going to do something about it.

So I was still quite elated as I rang my mother in Galway to share the news. I only ever rang home on Saturdays so she knew there was something up as soon as I rang on a Friday.

"Hi Mam."

"What's wrong?"

"I'm in the hospital in Bremen."

"You're what? What's happened? Are you OK?"

"I'm grand, but I have a brain tumour. It's fine though; they're operating on me tomorrow, and they're taking it out."

There was silence on the other end of the phone as my mother tried to process the bombshell I'd dropped on her.

"You're fecking joking," she said.

Deutsche B.A.'s staff members were incredible and organised all her flights at short notice. Dad drove Mam to Shannon Airport where she flew to Heathrow to catch a connecting flight to Bremen. She reached the hospital the next morning just before the surgery.

She discovered that devoted Anja was already by my bedside. I was red-faced as Anja continued to smother me with sympathy and endearments. I tried to explain the sequence of events that led me to the hospital, but Anja clung to my hand, felt my brow, smoothed my hair, and pecked my cheek with kisses.

"The poor thing, you wouldn't believe what he's been through the last few weeks," she told Mam. "I've been doing my best to look after him, but he's been through a terrible time. I've been sick with worry. I'm so upset about all this. "

I could see my mother looking from me to this middle-aged woman and wondering: "What on earth is going on here?"

Anja didn't want to leave my side for a minute, but I assured her I'd be OK now that my mother was here.

"Don't worry, I'll be back soon," she said kissing and hugging me again before she bustled away. My mother didn't bat an eyelid.

"Lovely woman. How long do you know her?"

I was afraid that she believed we were a couple.

"I only work with her!"

I imagined I could see a quizzical look on Mam's face.

"I really don't know what all the kissing and touchy-feely stuff is about! She brought me to the hospital but now she won't go away!"

That settled it as far as I was concerned. I couldn't have anyone thinking I was going out with Anja. I knew what I had to do. I asked for a pen and paper and then summoning all my powers of concentration, I wrote her a letter. It read something like:

"Dear Anja,

I want to thank you from the bottom of my heart for all your help and support over the last few weeks. I don't know if I could have survived without you.

However, I'm concerned that a misunderstanding has arisen between us.

I want you to know that I will always be your friend, but I am not your boyfriend and never will be. I would appreciate if you would not hold my hand in public or engage in other inappropriate displays of affection, as it may lead people to the wrong conclusion about our relationship.

I will be forever grateful for all you have done for me, and I hope we can always remain good friends."

I know I signed it: "Lots of love, John."

Don't ask me why I wrote a letter like that. To be fair, I had a brain tumour, and I wasn't thinking straight. I was immature, and I couldn't bear anyone thinking I would go out with a woman old enough to be my mother. The letter was part cowardice too, of course, because I knew I couldn't say it to Anja's face. I put the letter in an envelope and placed it by my bed to give to her.

The surgeon, Dr Elke Fischer, arrived, armed with my most recent scans, to discuss the surgery. My mother always says that once she flew out of Heathrow, she hardly heard anyone speak English again for weeks. Unlike cities like Berlin and Frankfurt, few Germans in Bremen speak English with any fluency.

Dr Fischer didn't speak any English, and my mother doesn't have a word of German, so I translated. The surgeon was blunt. She said the surgery would be long and challenging due to the position of the tumour. The brain stem is a very delicate area that controls many vital body functions. She said there were many risks and many possible complications.

I asked, straight out, what chance did I have of surviving the operation.

"Funfzig-funfzig," she said. She gave me a 50-50 chance.

"Ich nehme das!" I replied. "I'll take it!"

I never felt the fear that most people would feel on hearing they have a brain tumour. I think all my fear was all used up in the weeks before the diagnosis. Just a few days ago, I believed I was about to die; now I had a chance of living.

Being a glass half-full kind of person, a 50-50 prognosis was excellent. I was perfectly confident that I was going to be OK. My mother mustn't have felt quite so confident because her face fell on hearing this translation.

The surgeon also warned that the recovery could be long and difficult and that I may face an extended hospital stay and rehabilitation.

I nodded at her thoughtfully but was thinking to myself: 'You don't know John Walsh. You don't know what you're talking about.'

In my mind, I was invincible, immortal, and my superhero strength would return as soon as this tumour was removed.

I was thinking, "I'll be out of this place in a week, Lady. Then I'll go back to work and resume my life like this never happened."

Anja was back by my bedside by the time I was about to be wheeled down for the surgery. She was tearful, clingy, and fussing over my gown and blanket.

I was cringing and desperate to make it clear to my mother that there was nothing between us. I handed Anja the letter as she was going.

She looked at the envelope and hugged and kissed me again, and her eyes were moist with tears.

Smiling tenderly down at me, she took the letter and clutched it to her chest.

"Don't worry, I'll always be here for you," she said.

It was the last thing Anja ever said to me.

OPERATION ANGST

The surgical team removed a golf ball-sized tumour from my head in, what turned out to be, a marathon 10.5-hour procedure. I never anticipated the level of pain that I was to experience afterwards.

For the first day or two, I came in and out of consciousness, and could only groan in agony. My head felt like it was going to split from the racking pain. The bandages wrapped mummy-style around my head seemed to be the only things holding my entire skull together.

As I gradually emerged from the post-surgery fog, it came as a shock that I felt far worse than I did before the surgery.

My whole body was immersed in pain as every part of me ached. My legs were like leaden-weight jelly that dragged me to the floor when the nurses tried to take me out of bed. My speech, when I could remember any words, was slurred and incoherent.

Tubes appeared to be coming out of everywhere. I had shunts and drainage tubes coming out of my head to drain away the fluid build-up. There were drips for antibiotics and intravenous fluids, a tube down my nose, a catheter into my bladder and other attachments linking me to monitors.

They had warned me about the risks of seizures, strokes, blood clots, bleeding, comas and infection. They should have warned me about the pain.

There was no relief from it. I couldn't sleep; I couldn't lie down, and I couldn't sit up. They couldn't give me enough pain relief and nothing they gave me seemed to work.

Several times the medics started me on new forms of pain relief. They'd tell me to be patient; that it could take two hours to kick in. Invariably, it didn't work so I'd wait for a couple of hours for a doctor to come down and assess me for a new drug. And that one didn't work either.

My speech was affected so it was a struggle to find the words to articulate the pain. My mother found it impossible to communicate too as no one in the hospital spoke English. I remember pressing the bell by the bed a lot and not understanding why they were torturing me.

Even when they knew what I wanted, they shrugged and walked away.

"We gave you pain relief two hours ago, we can't give you any more," became a familiar refrain.

I was like a caged animal that had been set alight.

In hindsight, I was a victim of bad pain management because now I know it's not the typical experience after brain surgery.

But for the first two weeks after that surgery, I was in such agony that I couldn't engage with anyone or anything.

It was so intense that I didn't worry about the other problems I was experiencing, including the fact that my legs no longer worked. Even though I could feel them, I could no longer control them.

Very quickly after the operation, they tried to make me get out of bed as it helps recovery and reduces the risks of blood clots.

The nurses and my mother would encourage me to sit at the side of the bed first and then attempt to get me into a chair. The physios would urge me to wiggle my toes. But that required concentration and the headaches were so severe I just wanted to stay in bed and die. I didn't want to know. I was deep down a dark tunnel of suffering, and I was no help to anyone including myself.

Weeks of trauma before the operation, and the severity of the pain after surgery, left me exhausted. I started to feel depressed for the first time in my life.

Throughout this time, I lay in a white and sterile high dependency ward that had one large window and contained two stainless steel beds and side lockers. There were no actual doors to the ward just a big wide frame where doors should have been.

I shared the ward with one other patient called Thomas. Slightly older than me, he was around 30 years old, and also had a brain tumour removed.

I was in the first bed when you entered the room, and Thomas was down by the window. It was quite a few weeks before I was in any mood to look out the window. Then I discovered I hadn't been missing anything apart from a view of the car park.

Thomas made a quick recovery and disappeared within two weeks of my surgery. From then on, it was just me fending off a never-ending stream of well-intentioned medics and my mother.

Mam made it her mission to get me out of bed every day no matter how bad I felt. Being a nurse herself, she knew the importance of movement and made sure I stuck to the doctors' exercise plans even if it meant she had to drag me.

"John, don't make it any harder than it already is," she'd warn. "I know you're in pain, but it's not going to get any better unless you get out of bed and move. The sooner you do this, the sooner you can get back into bed. Let's get it over with and move!"

She was also determined for me to maintain some level of hygiene because I certainly didn't care. She and the nurses would use a wheelchair to get me into a shower room and shuffle me into a seat under the showerhead. Then they'd turn on the shower and hear me roar as even a trickle of water falling on my head was excruciating. Water boarding seemed like a kinder alternative to washing my hair.

Around this time there was a discussion about moving me to Switzerland for rehabilitation. The doctors hadn't expected so many post-operative complications.

They discussed transferring me to a centre in Geneva, Switzerland that specialises in rehab for people with brain injuries. They believed six weeks there could provide the intensive physio I required.

In the meantime, they sent me to their physio department on a week's trial. A young, energetic therapist called Peter gave me physio every day. I responded so well that they decided I didn't need to travel after all.

"The feeling will come back into your legs once you get them moving again," said Peter. "It's going to be hard at first but, believe me, you won't know yourself in a few weeks if you put in the effort now."

In the beginning, I couldn't stand at all. I needed the support of a harness suspended from the ceiling to keep me upright. My arms were nearly as useless as my legs.

"Now put your arms on the horizontal bars and use them to help balance yourself," urged Peter.

"Hands...gone." I'd struggle to find the words to explain myself.

"Your arms are still weak, but you need to try and work them too. Try and grip the bars while we work on moving your legs."

The high-intensity pain nagged on mercilessly for two horrible weeks. Then the natural healing processes may have taken effect or the hospital got a handle on managing the pain but suddenly, the agony receded.

Life became bearable again. It was only then that I was able to fully engage with the physiotherapists and speech therapists.

I was red-faced, panting and covered in a layer of sweat after every session of physio. I never knew exertion like it.

Day-by-day, with Peter's constant pushing and encouragement, I started improving. We worked on things like coordination and strength. I remember the real sense of achievement that I felt when I learned to bounce a ball again.

The depression started to lift as I felt my mobility return. At last, I was making real progress so I pushed myself more and more.

For weeks I spoke with such a slurred voice that it sounded like I was drinking all day. My mouth couldn't form any words that began with an 'F' or 'S' and I couldn't remember the names of everyday items.

When the caterers forgot to put cutlery on my dinner tray one day, I could see a knife and fork in my head, but I couldn't remember those two simple words in either English or German. I was frustrated beyond belief. Every day was a game of Charades where I had to mime what I wanted to say.

With no shortage of facilities at the hospital, I received three or four hours of intensive speech therapy every day. Slowly, steadily, my speech and memory began to improve too.

It took another four weeks but then it all came together, and I began to walk with some confidence and speak with less hesitance again. The miserable, shuffling patient who was hunched over a steel walker was gradually transforming back into the vital, young person I was before the surgery.

My mother stayed in Bremen this whole time. She lived in my old apartment and got on better with the landlady, Hildegarde, than my former flatmate David or I ever did.

Meanwhile, David never really got over the night I had that seizure. He found it difficult battling with the language barrier in Bremen and he became disillusioned with Germany and the job so he went home.

After five long weeks of supervising her son's care, Mam felt I was doing so well that she could return to Ireland and resume her job and her life. My twin, Cathy, flew out to Bremen to take her place.

The doctors warned that I wouldn't be fit to return to work for months, but they said I could go home to Ireland to recover as soon as they released me from the hospital.

Meanwhile, the All-Ireland hurling final was hurtling towards me. The game was scheduled for September 10th, so I fixed on that date as a target. I decided to be home to watch the Croke Park final in the pub.

Once I focussed on an end date, it spurred me to work even harder in my rehab. I told the doctors that I wanted to go home, and I had to be signed out by September 9th.

By now, the consensus was that the tumour had gone, and I didn't need any further treatment. The hospital had identified the tumour as a rare and complex one. Because so few people had it, there was no real information and no research carried out on it.

The belief was that it was a 'low-grade' and 'indolent' or slow-growing tumour, and most likely, it was benign. Radiotherapy was ruled out. They decided there was no need for it with a liponeurocytoma.

There's a train of thought now among consultants that I should have had radiation to try and stop a recurrence.

After I returned home, my consultant David Allcutt, in Beaumont Hospital in Dublin questioned the Germans' confidence that the tumour would not recur.

David, who took over my case, sent a letter to University Hospital Galway in November 2000. In the letter, he said that he studied my files and said he understood that the tumour was a liponeurocytoma variant and a PNET or a Primitive Neuroectodermal tumour. He believed therapy might be advisable.

"The German doctors seem to feel that this carries a good prognosis and does not require any adjuvant therapy," he wrote. "However, my own understanding of PNETs is that they usually do tend to recur without adjuvant therapy. "

David requested an MRI scan of my brain and spinal cord and asked for all the slides and scans to be sent from Germany so he could review them. He also wrote to radiation experts for their views. Everyone confirmed the German doctor's views regarding post-operative treatment. All available information "indicated that this tumour is indeed a low-grade tumour and therefore doesn't require any additional adjuvant post-operative therapy."

The best medical opinion at the time deemed radiation unnecessary, but I have to wonder if they had erred on the side of caution at the time, would the rest of my life have been different?

Given a clean bill of health by my German doctors, I was discharged after seven full weeks in the hospital on September 9th. We didn't hang around. Cathy and I took a taxi straight to the airport and flew to London and then on to Shannon.

Looking frail, pale, with a vivid scar on the back of my head and a bit unsteady in my gait, I still felt on top of the world. When one of the cabin crew offered to get me a wheelchair at Shannon Airport, I was surprised. I hadn't felt as alive and as energetic in a long time.

Once I got home, I was exuberant and looked forward to watching the All-Ireland hurling finals in the local pub the next day.

My father didn't want me to go out, probably because he was afraid that I was too wobbly on my feet for a glass of Guinness.

But I was never so determined to do anything. That image of being in the pub for the All-Ireland finals was what drove me to get back on my feet and out of the hospital.

I remember walking into Sheridan's in Milltown that scorching September day and there was an immediate hush in the pub. Maybe people expected to see someone bald and in a wheelchair. I'm not sure what they were expecting, but it's clear they weren't expecting me to be in the pub watching the All-Ireland finals.

I remember one guy coming up to me and marvelling at my speedy recovery.

"If you fell into a barrel of s**t, you'd come out in a white suit!" he declared.

I thought the same thing myself that day as I watched Kilkenny beat Offaly in the All-Ireland hurling final.

I felt like an All-Ireland champion myself. I was home, and I had beaten a brain tumour.

NO PLACE LIKE HOME

After seven weeks of life in a sterile German hospital, it was a relief to snuggle into the cosy, security blanket of home.

"It's only temporary," I told everyone. "I'm going back to Germany as soon as the doctors say I'm fit for work again."

Given that I've only fond memories of growing up in Liskeavy, it was wonderful to be back among the familiar and the welcoming.

The landscape around our home is flat, lush and green and surrounded by miles of stone walls, hedgerows, brooks and rivers. It's rural, pastoral countryside where sheep farming is common.

You can see as far as Croagh Patrick in County Mayo on a clear day. The only other elevated ground in the area is the site of an ancient fortress known as Cnoc Meadha. Around 11 miles from home, it's said to be the burial spot of Maeve, the legendary Queen of Connaught.

Our house is located in a place some people might describe as 'the middle of nowhere'. There are big tufts of grass growing down the middle of the winding country lane that ends at our house. The nearest shop is a drive of 3 miles in the village of Milltown. The market town of Tuam, where I went to school, is 10 miles away. The bright lights of Galway city are 27 miles distant, and the coast is almost 30 miles away.

After all the time spent confined to a hospital ward, I marvelled at the vast space around me again. Liskeavy is all big open skies with scudding clouds and an endless patchwork of green fields to the horizon. Growing up, I felt a sense of freedom and of endless possibilities in our remote surroundings.

As a twin, I'm the eldest of six children by a matter of minutes. My sister Cathy and I had the undivided attention of our mother, Carmel, a district nurse and our dad, Patrick, an electrician with the ESB, for just two years. Then my twin sisters Laura and Linda arrived followed by the youngest sister Alma and younger brother, Padraic.

It was a hectic household with just over six years between the oldest and the youngest of our family. My mother recalls when our living room was crammed with three playpens and her days were filled with endless nappy changes and bottle feeds.

By all accounts, I was a fun-loving, hyperactive child who fell into all sorts of mischief. One of my earliest memories is one of my worst childhood misdemeanours. I was only around three years old when my father came home with a brand new, red Ford Escort car. We all gathered around and gazed in admiration at his shiny new motor.

A day or two later, I must have been bored playing in a sandpit in the garden. Bucket and spade in hand, I decided to further explore the new car.

I somehow managed to unscrew the cap to the car's petrol tank. It came to me that this hole in the side of the car would be an ideal place to put my sand. I began carefully pouring my bucket of sand into the petrol tank.

Suddenly, my mother came running at me from the house, screaming at me from the top of her lungs.

"John! Jesus Christ, John! Get away from that car!"

I dropped the bucket as Mam charged towards me and howled with fright. I still managed to get half a bucket into the petrol tank before being interrupted.

The car that Dad had driven from the garage less than a week ago wouldn't even start. He called a mechanic who removed the petrol and sand, washed out the fuel tank and filled it up with clean fuel again.

But Dad's brand new car was never the same, and it chugged its way down country roads before he got rid of it.

If I never learned from my mistakes, neither did the people around me. They were always leaving things lying around for me to break.

My dad made the mistake of leaving his hammer unattended one day. After an hour observing him hammering and sawing at an old shed door, I decided to do the same myself. Unfortunately, I decided to hammer our fully glazed patio door. As soon as I landed the hammer, the entire door shattered down around me.

Mam and Dad came running and once reassured that I was alive, they threatened to kill me.

"Touch that hammer again and I'll murder you!" said my mother. "Don't touch anything that doesn't belong to you, do you hear me?"

Dad just took a deep breath, shook his head and walked away. He made a 20-mile round trip to Tuam town to pick up another pane of glass and then spent the following hour and a half fixing it into place.

By now, everyone's temper had cooled so I returned from the shadows to watch my dad at work again. Minutes after he stood back to inspect his completed work, I spotted the hammer again. My three-year-old brain vaguely remembered something about not touching it, but the allure of the tool proved irresistible.

Hammer in hand, I decided to give the glass such a little tap that no one would even notice. Instead, there was an almighty crash and for the second time in a matter of hours, my parents found their startled child surrounded by a sea of broken glass.

This time, my dad went berserk. I scarpered as fast as my chubby little legs could carry me. I fled, where I always did when I was in big trouble, to my granny's.

My paternal grandmother, Nelly Walsh's house was located 50 yards away on the same road. Nelly was my sanctuary and protection. Her love was unconditional. It didn't matter what I did because, in her eyes, I could do no wrong. Not everyone else was of the same opinion so I spent a lot of time there.

After school each day, I also went straight to my granny's. I was one less handful for our neighbour to mind until Mam got home from work.

The lynchpin of Nelly's social life was playing cards. Neighbours and friends gathered at her house every Monday and Friday night to play Twenty-Five. The card games, which required a combination of luck and skill to win, began each night at 9.00pm sharp. Everyone played for money even if the stake was only a few pence.

Aged just 9 or 10, you'd find me stuck in the middle of a bunch of 70 and 80-year-old card players and loving every minute of it. All were lifelong Pioneers so no one touched alcohol during card nights. They were hardened tea drinkers instead and because I was the most mobile in the house, I was the designated tea-maker and server.

But I also got to play, and I was soon as avid a player as my granny. It helped that I never lost money on card night. My grandmother or her friends would top me up again and always made sure I wasn't out of pocket before I went home.

Nelly's husband and my granddad, Patrick Walsh, died when I was just 6-years-old. He led a fascinating life during one of the darkest and most turbulent periods of Irish history, so I wish I had the chance to really get to know him.

He was born to a farming family in Liskeavy, just like his father before him, on July 12th, 1899.

Joining the Irish Volunteers in 1917, he later held the rank of battalion commandant in the old IRA.

As a member of the Milltown Company of the Irish Volunteers, he was involved in two ambushes on Royal Irish Constabulary patrols from Milltown Barracks in 1921. Sergeant Morrin and Constable Day were killed in the second attack on June 27, 1921.

The Black and Tans dragged him out of mass one Sunday and lined him up to shoot on Milltown Bridge. Family lore has it, that he back-flipped over the bridge into the Clare river and escaped.

He later sailed for America from Cobh and he lived there for eight years before returning.

Granddad's 1983 funeral remains vivid in my mind even though I was very young because he was buried with full military honours. His coffin was draped in the Tricolour and an Irish Army firing party gave a gun salute over the coffin.

My grandmother, who was 20 years younger than her husband, remained a constant and much-loved presence all through my childhood until her death fourteen years later.

There were 7 boys and 12 girls, including my twin sister Cathy, in my first class in Milltown National School in 1981.

My four sisters and I used to cycle a half a mile to meet the bus heading to Milltown. We threw our unlocked bikes into the ditch, boarded the bus and picked them up later on our way home.

My school attendance was impeccable but my school reports were less outstanding. While I'd say I was a bright child, school for me was all about socialising and general entertainment.

After Milltown, I went to St Jarlath's Secondary School in Tuam where nearly all the teachers were priests.

I was a day boy surrounded by hundreds of students, from all around the country, who were boarders. All 600 of us knew each other only by nickname. I was Welly, and I went to school with guys called Scan, Mama T, Del Boy and Bosco and other names too rude to mention.

Besides German, the only other school subject in St Jarlath's that interested me was art. At the end of my first year, I was told I'd have to choose either music or art to study for the Junior Cert. But there was no doubt in my mind that I'd study art forever.

I loved art class because you could chat as you worked making it the perfect subject for a social butterfly like me. I quite fancied myself as an artistic talent too. For a full school term, I believed I sketched like Da Vinci and painted like Picasso. I was delighted with myself.

It turns out my enthusiasm for the subject was let down by a complete lack of talent. When my school report arrived, it was missing an art grade but was accompanied by a thoughtful note: 'John should consider music for his Junior Cert.' I was gutted.

Sport was my greatest extracurricular passion. Any sport would do. For two entire days, I was glued to the telly watching Denis Taylor and Steve Davis battle it out for the 1985 Snooker World Championship title.

Taylor was given little chance of winning, but he hung in there all day Saturday and all through Sunday. The much-vaunted Davis raced into a clear lead on the Sunday night and just needed one more frame to win the match.

That was the exact time I was packed off to bed. My parents told me to forget the snooker; I had school in the morning.

Of course, Irishman Denis Taylor caused a major shock by making a comeback in the early hours of Monday morning in one of the most celebrated sporting finals of all time.

Next day at school, the lads were elated.

"You see that final last night? Something else wasn't it?" said one.

"Yeah, Steve Davis hammered him!" I said still unaware that sporting history had taken place after my bedtime.

Not only had I missed one of the greatest sporting moments ever, but I was red-faced because all the lads knew I'd been put to bed.

By the time I was 8-years-old, I was already mad into G.A.A. but hadn't discovered premiership soccer. That changed in 1985 when I accepted a bet from a die-hard Manchester United fan at school.

"I bet you 50p that Man U will win the FA Cup Final against Everton," he said.

"I bet you they won't," I said.

I hadn't any interest in or knowledge of Manchester United or Everton, but because there was 50p involved, I watched the match.

Man United won 1-0 courtesy of a Norman Whiteside goal, and that was it. I was hooked on soccer and Manchester United from that day. I've been a devoted Red Devils fan ever since.

G.A.A. will always be my first love, though. My uncle Gabriel brought me to my first hurling final in 1987 where I was beside myself to see Galway beat Kilkenny by 4 points.

Captained by a young full back, Conor Hayes, that team boasted a famous half back line of Peter Finnerty, Tony Keady and Gerry McInerney.

My uncle and I stood in the goals in Croke Park after the match and marvelled at how big they were. Staring up in awe at these sporting giants, I wanted to be one of them too.

More than anything else in the world, I wanted to have 80,000 people cheering for me in Croke Park. Galway football was in the wilderness then, but I remember that day dreaming of being the man to turn the entire team's fortunes around.

St Jarlath's school lavished attention on those who excelled at football or academia, but I was lazy on both scores.

The school was renowned for its passion for football and was an academy for GAA superstars at the time. You had to be exceptionally committed and talented to be on the team.

All I ever wanted when I was younger was to play for Galway. I imagined I was a legendary Galway player of old like Gay McManus or Noel Tierney.

Even though I was mad for football, I didn't want to put in the work. The tedious bits like training in the cold and the rain were not for me. I wanted to get straight to the action and play in Croke Park.

I hadn't any focus or anyone to kick me in the backside. St Jarlath's teachers were encouraging rather than disciplinarians, so it was easy for me to put my feet up and socialise for five years in secondary school.

My mother reminds me of one school report which read: "John could do much better if he spent less time engaging with the lesser lights." I was never quite sure who or what the 'lesser lights' were.

But where football was concerned, it was an exciting time to be in St Jarlath's in the early 90s even as a non-player. Year after year, we witnessed the most incredible team of players hone their talents until they played like a symphony orchestra on the field. You could sense something big was happening.

The school reached the finals of the All-Ireland College Championships known as The Hogan Cup near the end of my first year at St Jarlath's in 1990.

Our hearts were racing, as we were one point down to St Patrick's College, Maghera in the last minutes of the game.

Then St Jarlath's Derek Duggan got a free kick and Karl Keirns punched the ball into the back of the net. We screamed at each other until we were red in the face. We were swept away on a wave of euphoria and boyhood hysteria. We'd won the Hogan Cup final!

Minutes later, we discovered that the referee had blown the full-time whistle just before the goal and we'd actually lost.

Our faces fell, and we stared at each other in silent disbelief. More than a few of us had to wipe away the fat tears that rolled down our cheeks. We were devastated, truly devastated.

But by 1994, we knew we had the most formidable college football team in the country. There was no one to touch St Jarlath's senior team.

Half the school went to the bookmakers at the beginning of the year and got 5/1 odds of winning the Hogan Cup. Our winnings were only the icing on the cake as our schoolmates stormed to victory that year. For the first time in a decade, we really had won the Hogan Cup.

Many on that winning Hogan team went on to the senior county level and turned around the fortunes of Galway football. They included Padraic and Tommy Joyce, John Divilly, Michael Donnellan, Declan Meehan and Tomas Meehan. John Haran went from St Jarlath's back to Donegal to star in their senior team.

Padraic, Michael and Declan were also winners of various Player of the Year awards.

When no one thought Galway had a hope of winning, I watched my schoolmates win the All-Ireland final against Kildare in 1998. I have to admit I shed a tear in the stands of Croke Park that day.

I was there again to watch the same bunch of lads win the final against Meath in 2001 again.

However, the focal point of our Hogan Cup team, John 'Scan' Concannon, who was arguably the best footballer of them all, was the one who never made it to senior level.

He should have been one of the legends of Galway football but John admitted years later that he didn't like training and didn't put in the commitment required.

When I hear people complain about the boredom of small town life or about feeling trapped in small, rural communities, I can't understand it.

Life in Liskeavy and its surroundings was never dull or claustrophobic to me. There was always something going on and wonderful people to engage with.

There's a great quality of life thanks to the close sense of community and good neighbours. There are the big wide skies, the carpet of stars on a clear night, all that fresh air and clear country roads.

At the same time, career opportunities are limited in a rural area, and when I first set out for Germany, I was eager to see what the rest of the world had to offer.

I had a lust for travel and was starry-eyed about the adventure of big city living.

However, as I made a gradual recovery from the brain tumour surgery, the prospect of returning to Germany didn't seem quite so attractive

I felt far less excited about going back the second time. But I was given a clean bill of health by December 2000 and there wasn't any real excuse for me to stay home any longer.

ALL OVER THE PLACE

My goal was to be back working in Germany within three months. I didn't realise how quickly the months would fly, and it seemed like no time had elapsed before I had to go back.

Deep down, I was reluctant to return but turning my back on an excellent job didn't make any sense. There was nothing for me in Galway.

There was a brief window, after I first came home, that I felt elated and triumphant. I felt like a champion; someone who had beaten a lethal brain tumour. I was also cheered by all the get-well cards and Mass cards that flowed in from all corners of the country.

"Couldn't be better! I'm flying!" I told everyone who enquired about my health.

It was true too; I was flying. During that time, the little things that once bothered me didn't annoy me anymore. I had a new perspective on life. I felt elated and strong again, and everything seemed to make sense to me. I felt like a lucky man.

But that initial euphoria and lightness began to fade after a few weeks. A sense of low-level depression and a gnawing anxiety took its place. Life seemed to become a bit darker and heavier. I stopped flying and crashed.

I fought off the gloom by walking miles of country roads. I began to look forward to long walks especially in the dark of night. The wilder, windier and wetter the night, the more I was drawn outside. I'd walk in the kind of weather that you wouldn't put out a cat, but I was alone in the elements and away from everything. I paced in the howling wind and driving rain and beneath the menacing silhouettes of swaying trees for months that winter.

By the time it was time to return to work, I had very mixed feelings. On the one hand, I was grateful to Deutsche B.A. who had been decent enough to keep my job open for almost six months since the surgery. I wanted to get back and prove that they hadn't made a mistake in hiring me.

I also yearned to live like a normal person again. I wanted to get up in the morning, go to work, have some structure in my life and start to make a living again.

On the other hand, even though I had recovered physically, mentally, I felt far from my old confident self. I was an entirely different person to the man I was six months earlier.

Emotionally, I was still all over the place, feeling unsettled and a bit forlorn. It felt like someone snatched my old fun-loving and high-energy personality and turned down the dimmer switch.

But if anyone had asked me, I wouldn't have been able to put my finger on what was troubling me.

Unlike the last time I was in Dublin airport, there was no beaming smile for the attendant at the gate. I was feeling far more apprehensive going to Germany the second time.

Almost as soon as I landed back in Bremen, I knew returning was a big mistake. Hellish memories of my months in Germany started rushing back, and there was no longer the option of outrunning the gloom on country roads every night.

That first morning, looking up at the ultra-modern facade of my workplace, I felt a sense of dread instead of the jubilance I'd hoped to feel. I realised I didn't want to be there, but I felt I had no option but to stick it out.

I told myself I was being totally irrational. I was lucky to have employers as understanding as Deutsche B.A. who'd kept my job open all these months. I was cured, and now I needed to resume my life and get over myself.

I had no grounds for complaint. My former workmates and bosses couldn't have been more welcoming, and there was an air of celebration upon my return.

I was brought straight back into the team, and everyone came over to shake my hand, slap me on the back and to enquire about how I was feeling. Everyone did their best to make me feel at home again. Everyone, that is, except Anja.

It really bothered me that I hadn't spoken to my co-worker and friend since I handed her that letter. In the intervening months, I began to doubt myself and wondered if I'd been mistaken about her having romantic illusions about us.

Aged 6, carrying a wreath behind my grandfather's coffin, Kilgevrin Cemetery, Milltown.

Walsh siblings: Padraic, Linda, Laura, Cathy, me, and Alma.

Me as an aspiring Galway player, aged 11.

Walsh family wedding photo: Laura, Linda, my mother Carmel, the groom (me), Padraic, my father Patrick (RIP), Alma and Cathy. *(Photographer: Sinéad Ní Riain)*

Smiles all around (thankfully) as Edel and I announced our engagement to Edel's parents, Josephine and Michael Tobin.

My sister-in-law Bríd, family friend Lorraine, Edel, sister-in-law Joan, and me as a stand-in bridesmaid at my sister-in-law, Marie's wedding in 2006.

Our bridal party: Padraic, Marie, Edel, me, Cathy and Fergal. *(Photographer: Sinéad Ní Riain.)*

Inset: Bald patch from radiation.

Edel and me on our wedding day. *(Photographer: Sinéad Ní Riain.)*

Selfie of Edel and me, taken on a trolley in A&E of UHG as we waited for an ambulance transfer to Beaumont Hospital, June 2010.

Feeling very unwell around Fírinne's birth.

Me and my brother, Padraic with new-born Fírinne.

Still on treatment and feeling emotional at Fírinne's christening.

Me with Edel and Fírinne in NYC for a consult with Memorial Sloan Kettering Hospital, 2012.

8,27+   20.9.14   10,800.00
                   2,510.89

Edel needs To stop on day off
① photocopy & post Receipts ☑
                              peter
② obseshys ALL for one Mirk
⑱ put Cde key Gift, / ☑
   on Pic
③ Spend time with Boot turts ☑
⑳B WKd on Fridge Door
④ Put clothes away ☑

⑤ Sort out old clothes
   in black bags
6
        Shopping for week
        Don't forget bags £2 Coin
⑦ Calculate how much we
need exactly for Edel C ☑
   + I need £150 in a/c for moetge Sep pay
⑧ £2,300 needs to come off
cu by + Christmas & clear too
       + 6k
⑨ Check with Revenue 2013
                       obsesh
⑩ Mow Genss ☑
⑪ Sick leave Record Rtn /
⑫ Hair cut (Sides).

Example of one of the many 'To Do' lists from my time on steroids.

Operation Houdini syndicate after a win at the Galway Races.

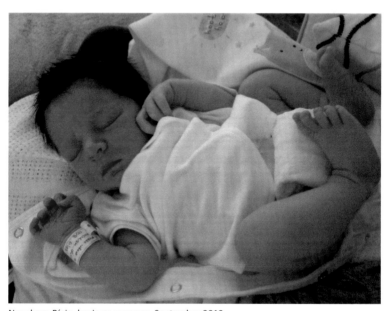

New-born Ríain, having a rare nap, September 2013.

Maybe I had overreacted. Maybe I'd been acting like a head case and had misinterpreted everything. I was racked with guilt because she had done so much for me.

In the weeks and months since the operation, I was too embarrassed to pick up the phone and try to resolve the matter. Instead, I hoped that by the time I returned to the office, she'd put everything that happened behind her.

I imagined she'd say 'John, great to see you!' and I'd say 'Great to see you, Anja!' and we'd make up again. It didn't happen that way.

We worked on different floors but every time we happened to meet in the corridor, she blanked me.

If I saw her across a crowded room and I attempted to approach her, she refused to make eye contact. She behaved like I didn't exist. Today they refer to it as 'ghosting'. To me, it was just the stone cold, silent treatment.

I'd never fallen out with anyone in my life like that, and I felt awful about it. Anja had been so kind to me. She had dropped everything to bring me to the hospital. She kicked up such a rumpus that she shamed the hospital into conducting proper tests for the first time.

She had saved my life, and I repaid her by hurting her so deeply that she refused to speak to me again.

Still, if I had my time all over again, I wouldn't change much about what I did. Anja's reaction to my letter leads me to believe I didn't misinterpret anything.

But I should have spoken to her rather than write a letter or maybe I should have worded the letter more sensitively. If I'd known just how hurt she'd be, I would have been more careful.

The Anja calamity was just another pressure I didn't want to deal with when I got back to Germany. Also by the time I returned, my former flatmate, David Lynch, had already gone home. Another guy at BA, Adrian King, invited me to stay in a spare room in his place instead. Hailing from Leeds in the UK, Adrian couldn't have been nicer.

"Look, the room is there, and it's empty," he said. "Stay as long as you like or until you find somewhere else you'd prefer to stay. We're on opposite shifts anyway, so we'll never see each other."

All the same, I missed the easy companionship and the common interests that I shared with David. It was early December now and the days were darker and the weather was colder. The atmosphere between Anja and me was ice cold. Germany was a lonelier, gloomier place when I returned.

There was something else missing too. I felt like more than a brain tumour had been taken out of me three months earlier.

It was a different John Walsh who returned to Germany. This version was an imposter who wore a mask so he looked exactly like the old John Walsh. But this one felt completely different. He was trapped in an invisible bubble, feeling distant and isolated from everyone.

From being a people-loving extrovert before the brain tumour, I was now withdrawn and found it harder to engage with those around me.

I'd always had a particular image of Germany and it fulfilled all my expectations when I got there first. The job and the lifestyle were everything I ever wanted. But now I felt like another person who was transported back to another lifetime. Everywhere I went, I was assailed by bad memories.

I've learned since that even if you've never had depression in the past, having a brain tumour can change all that.

Learning that you have a life-threatening condition is a body shock in itself. That kind of bad news alone can trigger feelings of anxiousness and depression.

There are also physical reasons why having a brain tumour can cause personality changes. The tumour itself, because of its position, can cause physical changes to the brain causing side effects like mood change.

It's inevitable that surgery of any kind, especially an invasive procedure on the brain, will have its own side effects.

Meanwhile, treatments like chemo and steroids can impact on the chemistry of the brain.

In fact, if you don't feel any depression after diagnosis and treatment for a brain tumour, you are probably in the minority.

Yet I was never warned that this might happen in any conversation with the medical profession. And when I got depressed, I didn't actually recognise it, understand it or know what to do about it.

I didn't know what was wrong with me except everything felt wrong. The last place I wanted to be at that time was in this strange environment where I'd experienced the worst days of my life.

No one would ever have realised this in Deutsche B.A. My work record when I returned was exemplary and my supervisor scored my performance as excellent. The quality and speed of my work probably improved because I felt that I had something to prove.

I also had a point to prove to my old GP Dr Wolfgang Voertig-Hoffman. I got a certain satisfaction when I asked him to update my medical file. He visibly winced when I told him I had been suffering from a brain tumour rather than panic attacks.

I hoped that he'd never be dismissive of anyone unlucky enough to present with the same symptoms again.

I went back to that church that I had gone to in the depths of despair and managed to find and thank the priest who had shown such kindness to me that day.

I also went back to see Dr Elke Fischer, the surgeon who removed the tumour, to thank her for everything she had done.

I hadn't shown much in the way of gratitude to her after the operation because I was in such pain afterwards.

I think my real mission going back to Germany was to say goodbye. I didn't know it at the time but I was really seeking to close the door on that dark episode of my life.

I made up my mind just three weeks after returning to Germany. I picked up the phone and called home.

"Mam, I want to come back. This isn't working out. I don't want to be here anymore."

She wasn't surprised, and she didn't try to change my mind.

"Come home so, John. We never wanted you to go in the first place. I never thought you were ready to go back anyway."

She realised there was something amiss with me before I did.

I couldn't bear any explanations, interrogations or farewells in Germany. I didn't tell a soul that I was leaving. I just booked my flight and counted down the days to the end of the week.

That Friday, I finished up at work as usual and wished everyone a good weekend.

After I had left, I sent an email to the personnel department in Deutsche B.A. to explain I wouldn't be back on Monday. I thanked them but said that I realised I wasn't ready to go back to work and wouldn't be back to work in Germany. In the light of everything that happened, I felt that Germany wasn't meant for me.

That night as Adrian was leaving for an evening shift, my bag was already packed in the room ready to go. I didn't have the heart to tell even him that I was going home.

So I sent him an email too which read something like "Thank you so much for everything, and goodbye." I tried to explain that I wasn't able for Germany or Deutsche B.A. anymore, but I'm sure he didn't understand any of it. I didn't understand it myself.

It's taken me all these years to know that it takes a long time to recover from brain surgery. It takes a whole lot longer than it takes the wound in your head to heal.

I didn't feel myself when I got back to Germany, but I didn't recognise it as depression. I failed to identify the symptoms for years, so it was a long time before I ever attempted to tackle it.

All I know is that a small black cloud, which I'd never felt before, began hovering over me after Germany. At times, the moods became more pronounced and at times, they faded away but usually they just hung around, lurking in the background.

Even today, I can't say if it was one or several events that triggered the change in my personality.

The weeks that I spent ill and terrified while getting brushed off by the medical profession had a long-lasting impact on my mental wellbeing. I definitely suffered significant levels of post-traumatic stress disorder afterwards.

Of course, it's also possible that the tumour itself caused enough pressure on the brain that it altered my normal temperament.

Or given that I had ten hours of brain surgery, it's possible too that the operation had an impact on my mood and personality.

I know for certain that being semi-invalided by the surgery was a massive blow to me, a young guy, who previously believed he was invincible.

It could have been any or all of these events that irrevocably changed me. All I know for sure is that before the tumour or 'B.T.', I was carefree show-off, confident, brash and outgoing. After the tumour or 'A.T.', I was introverted, lost and melancholy. I felt like a loner for the first time in my life.

The demands of a dynamic, busy job surrounded by the buzz of energetic and upbeat colleagues were too much for me just then. It was with total relief that I boarded the plane for home. The German dream was over for me forever.

The only thing that remained unresolved in Germany was Anja. She was probably part of the reason I went home.

I still think of her today quite a lot. I'd like to thank her for saving my life, and I'd like to apologise for the way things ended between us.

I actually looked up the White Pages in Germany a year or so ago and found someone bearing her name. I rang the number and a woman answered. I wasn't sure it was Anja. I chickened out and put the phone down.

I didn't know where to start explaining.

EDELWEISS

The first time I heard Edel's name was the year before I went to Germany. After my first year of college, I quit a house share on the Headford Road in Galway and moved home for the summer.

My former housemate, Fergal O'Dowd, phoned me soon after to gloat.

"I've swapped you for a stunning blonde," he said.

"What are you on about, Fergal?"

"A gorgeous blonde has moved into your room."

"Where did you find a gorgeous blonde?"

"She's an architect, and she's just joined our firm. She's from Tipperary, and her name is Edel Tobin. Seriously, you want to see this girl; she's gorgeous! You'd definitely like her."

Fergal was fond of describing everything and everyone as "gorgeous". A day or two later, I dropped by the Headford Road to see my old pal. We both knew why I was really there.

They say it takes three seconds to make an impression, but it took less than that to make up my mind about Edel. As I stepped in the door of my former house share, I saw her descending the stairs.

She was blonde and willowy with alert blue eyes framed by a perfect face. I was smitten.

If I had a 'type', Edel was it. She was elegant, tall and striking; I thought she was perfect in every way.

Even the name Edel, from the rare Alpine flower, Edelweiss, was auspicious considering my love for all things German.

Even though I brimmed with youthful confidence back then, I felt this girl was out of my league. There was no way I could get this girl by being myself, I thought. Straight away, I felt I needed a game plan.

Desperate not to look desperate, I didn't even smile at her. Instead, I gave her an offhand nod and muttered something charming like: 'How's it going?'

She didn't give me a second glance as she left the house minutes later. That was it; our brief encounter was over.

When Fergal turned to quiz me, I tried to look indifferent. If I gave him even the slightest hint I was interested, the news would get back to her.

Fergal was the kind of guy who'd do anything to make his friends happy, including beg Edel to go out with me. I knew I wouldn't stand a chance with her then.

"Well, what do you think of her?" he asked. His eyes danced. He was pleased with himself.

"Isn't she gorgeous?"

I looked as if I didn't know who he was talking about.

"Oh, your new flatmate?" I shrugged. "She's all right, I suppose. I don't know why you were going on about her so much, though."

Fergal looked crestfallen, but he soon forgot about his hopes of making a match and turned to all the other news he had to discuss.

It turned out that faking disinterest wasn't a great game plan. Fergal's kind-hearted bid to fix up his single friend hadn't worked so he hardly mentioned Edel again.

As a result, I never heard where I might 'bump' into her or if she was going out with anyone else. I dropped into the house on the Headford Road on a few occasions, but Edel was never there. It was a whole year before I saw her again.

David Lynch and I planned a going-away party in April 2000 at the Skeffington Arms Hotel on Galway's Eyre Square. We were moving to Germany after landing jobs with Deutsche B.A.

Of course, Fergal was among those invited to the party, and Edel happened to tag along with him.

I hadn't directly asked her because I wasn't supposed to know who she was. Anyway, I figured there was no point trying to start something new when I was leaving the country.

I saw her the instant she swept into the Skeffington with her long, golden hair and her bright smile lighting up the room.

At the very end of the night, after I sank several pints of bravado, I swaggered over to her. She was putting on her coat and getting ready to leave.

I hadn't spoken a word to her in a year, but it didn't matter because I flashed my most irresistible smile. Beer always made me more smooth, suave and charming.

"Hi Edel," I said. "Where are we going tonight then?"

I thought she'd jump at the chance to leave with me for some reason. Edel looked me up and down before fixing me with a withering glare.

"I don't know about you, but I'm going home," she retorted.

Then she spun on her heel and walked out, taking all my boozed-up confidence with her. I felt as deflated as the burst party balloons around me.

There was no need for it, I thought. No need to be so bitchy. What a wagon. What a complete wagon!

But, oh my God, I fancied her even more now.

I didn't see Edel or have any contact with her again until the summer of 2001. It was ten months after I left Germany and moved back home. Physically, I looked fine. No one would have suspected anything was wrong by looking at me, but I wasn't coping mentally.

Before I went to Germany, I was a fury of energy and enthusiasm for everything that life had to offer. Now I felt listless and despondent and had no interest in anything. I moped around the house with no idea why I was feeling that way.

I was on disability allowance and working two nights a week as a barman in a hotel. All I could handle was two nights' work because I couldn't cope with any pressure or stress. My concentration levels were zero, my mood was low, and I could fly into a panic over the slightest thing.

Meanwhile, the tumour was gone; I was cured and it was time to move on and get over it but I couldn't. The outgoing and confident John Walsh who'd been around for 23 years had disappeared and a more troubled soul had taken his place. I only knew that I felt sad for no good reason.

By now, my friend Fergal had just broken up with another girl.

"I'm never going to meet anyone," he moaned. "I'm going to die alone."

I decided it was time to become Galway's answer to Cilla Black. So I arranged to meet my twin, Cathy, in the pub one night and just happened to bring along Fergal. As I suspected, they immediately clicked and now Fergal is my brother-in-law.

He repaid the favour by bringing Edel and me together for a third, more fortuitous meeting. It all started when he rang me at home one evening.

"Meet me in Galway on Thursday night," he said. "A guy I know has designed a new pub called Bazaar, and there are rumours of free drink. You might as well; you're doing nothing anyway on a Thursday night."

He added: "Make a real night of it and stay with Cathy and me."

Liskeavy was nearly an hour's drive from the city, so I was happy to take up his offer of a room. I had vague hopes that Edel might be there, but I didn't know for sure that she would. And I couldn't ask Fergal because that would have triggered awkward questions that I didn't want to answer.

I wasn't optimistic about my chances with her even if she did turn up. Our last encounter hadn't been encouraging, and I thought if she turned up at all, she'd probably have a boyfriend in tow.

It was July 12th, the public holiday in Northern Ireland, and the city was hopping with tourists from the north. I spotted Edel among a group of mutual friends as soon as I walked in the door of the pub.

Fate played a hand because the only available seat was next to her. I took it as a good sign that she didn't recoil as I sat in beside her.

"Hi Edel, how are you?"

"Fine thanks, John, how are you?"

She remembered my name. It had to be another positive sign. I soon had her cornered and we chatted to the exclusion of everyone around us.

I discovered Edel was raised in a farming family in a rural area outside Cashel in Tipperary. When I was having a brain tumour removed in Germany, she spent the year travelling around the world. She was 22-years-old, two years younger than me, and she studied architecture at UCD. She had moved to Galway to work in Simon J. Kelly & Partners. And I couldn't take my eyes off her as she talked.

Her smile had a shyness that gave me a warm glow inside and she was completely unaware of how lovely she was. Even though she was reserved, she was funny and easy to talk to.

Still unsure if she was just making polite conversation, I tested the water at times. I 'casually' touched her knee a few times to emphasise a point in the conversation. When she didn't brush away my hand, I took it as another encouraging sign.

I managed to pull Fergal aside at some stage.

"About Edel, is there anyone on the scene at the moment?" I asked with some urgency.

I didn't want to raise my hopes and then have them crushed when she announced that she had a boyfriend at the end of the night.

Fergal answered something like: "Who needs to know and what's it worth?"

There was a bit of unseemly wrestling behind Edel's back before he confirmed that she was single.

The next hurdle was to persuade her to see me again. A conversation arose about a charity fundraising dance taking place during the Galway Races at the end of the month. Fergal, my sister, and all their friends were going. In a carefully, casual tone, I asked Edel if she was going too.

"I've no one to go with," she replied.

That was my cue and the opportunity I'd been waiting for.

"Do you want me to go with you so?" I asked, shrugging as if I didn't mind doing her the favour.

When she replied "Yeah, fine," I did cartwheels in my head.

At last, I had secured a first date with Edel. My masterplan had worked, but it took a lot longer than I expected, as it was now two years since I'd first seen her on the stairs in Fergal's house on the Headford Road.

My face was one big beaming smile as I went back to Cathy and Fergal's that night. It had been a long time since I felt this happy.

Of course, Fergal wanted to know all about the budding romance with his workmate.

It had been my first and only real encounter with Edel but already I'd little doubt that she was the one for me. I didn't care when Fergal howled with laughter; I knew it was true.

"I think I'm going to marry that girl," I told him.

OBSESSION

Edel was so lovely that I was mad about her from our first meeting. But I was afraid that if I appeared too eager, I'd scare her off.

I was determined to move slowly and do everything right. There was a new me in town.

Fergal and a few friends from work arranged to meet for lunch the day after our fateful night in the pub. Edel had said she'd be there, but I figured it was too soon to see her again and somehow resisted the temptation to go. I didn't want to be jumping around her like an excited puppy.

Weeks later, she admitted that she was disappointed when she didn't see me walking in the door with Fergal for lunch that day. She had no idea how happy I was to hear her say that.

Instead, I went home that day, and I floated around like a lovesick teenager. My younger brother, Padraic, was the first to hear all about the new love of my life.

"Edel is so smart that she can do anything," I said. "She studied to be an architect. You have to be really smart to do that, you know. She plays the piano, and she has this fabulous singing voice. She's really easy to talk to, but you'd want to see her because she is drop dead gorgeous and she has this blonde hair that…"

I couldn't talk enough about Edel and her all round brilliance and gorgeousness. My 16-year-old brother sat looking at me with his mouth open. He'd never seen this before.

"Jesus, John," he said. "You're obsessed with that girl!"

When I finished boring Padraic, I rhapsodised about Edel to my mother.

"She's lovely and tall. She's the perfect height for me," I wittered. "She's the only girl I've gone out with that I don't have to bend down to kiss."

'Obsession' was too long a nickname so Padraic began using the abbreviation 'Obsesh' to refer to Edel. Soon everyone in the family called her that. It was: "Obsesh is on the phone!" and "Are you seeing Obsesh tonight?"

Of course, Edel soon learned about her pet name too. Another girl might have been alarmed that her boyfriend's obsession with her had become the family joke. Luckily, she thought it was hilarious because she's rarely called anything else now.

Edel's name came up on my phone today, and I answered as usual: 'Hi Obsesh!' Instead, it was my 4-year-old.

"It's not Obsesh, it's Fírinne!" she scolded.

But she knows her mother's pet name just like everyone else in the family.

'Obsesh' and I met for our first official date at the Galway Races later that month, and our grand reunion was a huge success. I remember she made her hat for the races, and I was impressed by her creativity. But then I was impressed by everything about Edel. We made each other laugh, and I found she was easy to be around.

From then on, we saw each other every chance we got. I still lived at home and she lived in a house share on the Headford Road but every spare minute was spent together or spent travelling to meet each other.

I adored her more with every passing day and by the end of the summer, Edel told me that she loved me too.

We were a couple; totally committed to each other. We were destined to be together forever. Then she dropped the bombshell.

"I'm moving back to Dublin for college next week," she said.

I was shocked.

"What college? What are you talking about? You're working now."

"Only for the summer. I thought you knew that."

I hadn't a clue. I didn't know that she was still at U.C.D. I just assumed she was qualified and working full-time.

I was devastated. Panic set in. The words "You can't leave me!" screamed in my head. Thinking back, I really was obsessed. I thought: "I can't let this happen; I want to be with this girl; I can't survive without her."

The next morning, I phoned Dublin City University to ask if they had a course of any description to suit this mature student. They told me they had a course in Applied Languages Spanish and German, but their classes were full. I wouldn't be able to start until the following year.

I spent the next year working part-time in the bar and jumping on the train to Dublin every chance I got. The year couldn't go fast enough. I moved into a house in Artane in September 2002 and became a college student again.

Of course, I did it for all the wrong reasons. I had no real interest in college; I just wanted to be close to Edel who, by now, had qualified. She was offered a job by the internationally renowned architectural firm, Heneghan Peng, and started working straight away in Dublin.

I was a much happier man now that Edel was in my life. I needed her a lot then, and I still do. I call her several times a day just to hear her voice. However, even Edel couldn't fix everything, and I still wasn't a hundred per cent right.

The depression was still there, and I was reckless, making rash decisions without thinking them through. My days were plagued by flashbacks and my nights, with nightmares. I had vivid visions of being wheeled into surgery again or being back in the surgery of my GP in Germany. Something on TV could trigger the memory of being in that eerie office with the psychiatrist, Dr Beckenbauer.

Every flashback made my anxiety levels soar and my stomach heave. My emotions were out of control at times, and I could be in the middle of a lecture and find myself crying for no reason at all. I was good at covering these incidents up saying I'd a bit of a cold or something in my eye. Still, even I was alarmed by my behaviour.

I'm a person who normally wears his heart on his sleeve, but I'd never spoken to anyone about the whole ordeal in Germany. My well-meaning mother had advised me to put everything that happened behind me.

"Get the word tumour out of your head," she said. "You're John Walsh; you're cured. It's in the past now, put it behind you and get on with your life."

At the same time, I knew I wanted to talk about it. I needed to talk about it.

Meanwhile, I wasn't applying myself to Applied Languages. I couldn't knuckle down or concentrate on anything. My head wasn't in the right place.

At one stage, I knocked on the door of the counsellor at college and sought professional help. The counselling helped to an extent but a day or two after each session, the blackness would return as bad as ever.

Edel never knew about my depression. I didn't tell her about the flashbacks, the nightmares or the crying. I felt too vulnerable back then. I thought if I told her she'd wonder what kind of a lunatic she was going out with.

If Edel said something like: "I don't think this is going anywhere," I would have fallen to pieces.

And I was good at masking my emotions. I perfected the art of feeling one way and portraying myself a different way. Sometimes, I went to bed congratulating myself on another Oscar winning performance. I felt every day was an act where I had to pretend to be normal.

The only thing good in my life was Edel. She was my crutch, and I depended so much on her for my mental and emotional well-being.

I wanted to settle down and get married. I was in a hurry to seal the deal, but practicalities like money and a job kept getting in the way.

Somehow I managed to pass the exams for the first year of college, but I started dropping out shortly after starting the second year.

Meanwhile, Edel was disciplined and focused. She notched up success after success in her academic life and her career.

Top of her year when she qualified from UCD in 2002, she went on to win the Thomas Ivory Medal for achieving the highest grade in the country in the Architectural Professional Registration Exam.

She was hired straight from college by a Dublin firm, Heneghan Peng Architects. A year later, she was on the team that beat 1,500 companies worldwide and won the hugely prestigious architectural commission to design the €300 million Grand Egyptian Museum beside the Giza pyramids in Cairo.

In 2004, she moved back to Galway and joined Simon J. Kelly & Partners Architects again where she's now a director.

Meanwhile, my career path wasn't quite so stellar. By 2004, I was still working two days a week as a barman in a local hotel, and I'd started another course as an accounting technician. I was struggling to find other work and move on in life.

From early on in our relationship, it was taken for granted between us that we were getting married. As far as I was concerned, spending the rest of our lives together was sorted after our first date.

Edel might have come around to the idea a little bit later but from then on, it was just about setting a date. The only reason we hadn't moved forward was because I felt I had little to offer. I wasn't in the place career-wise where I wanted to be.

But we were three years together now, and we were behind in our five-year plan. We don't have a five-year plan anymore or even a year-plan. Now it's one day at a time. But we had a plan then, and we were behind schedule on the engagement.

So we decided to get engaged. I never had second thoughts about marrying Edel; it was what I wanted more than anything else in the world. I was more concerned about what I could bring to this partnership. I kept thinking to myself, "What am I doing asking this girl to marry me? I've no right to ask her. I've no job, no money. I'm still studying. I've no idea what I'm doing."

But the process was moving forward, and the first order of business was to buy a ring. We went to three or four different jewellers, but Edel didn't see anything she loved. I exhaled a bit. It looked like selecting the ring would take ages. But then, we dropped into another jewellers' store, and suddenly she spotted the ring she had to have.

"This is it!" she said happily brandishing the diamond on her hand. "This is the one. Isn't it perfect?"

That wasn't my first thought. My first thought was "Oh sh*t, how am I going to afford that?"

Even though getting engaged is supposed to be a happy time in anyone's life, it wasn't as simple as that for me. It was a weird kind of time. I felt like I was under-achieving and didn't deserve such happiness.

Our engagement was never going to be a big surprise for Edel or anyone else. Wherever she was, I was. We'd been glued to each other for the past three years. For us, it was just about formalising our plans to marry. Everyone else was just waiting for us to get on with it too.

As soon as the ring was fully paid off, I invited Edel to the Glenlo Abbey Hotel, about two miles outside Galway for a night away. It was July 2004, and I thought that the gardens would provide a suitable setting for a formal proposal of marriage.

I toyed with the idea of renting a boat on Lough Corrib and proposing on the lake. But as I've a deadly fear of water, I scotched that idea. Instead, I approached the hotel concierge and asked him to point out the most romantic place on the grounds. He showed me a scenic stroll that would bring us down to a pretty lakeside view.

I wish I were the poetic sort who had rehearsed an epic proposal, but as Edel will testify, the big romantic gesture is not one of my talents.

Instead, I led her down to the lake and said something like: "Edel, there's something I want to ask you."

"What's wrong with you?" she said.

Because I was over-thinking the situation, I struggled to get the words out. I can't even remember if I got down on one knee. It was part of the initial plan, but my head was all over the place now.

"Do you still want to marry me?" I asked

Edel turned to look at me, and her face lit up with the most brilliant smile.

"Oh great, you've got the ring!" she trilled.

Her left arm remained fully extended in front of her face for the rest of the day as she admired her ring in every light.

ONE WEDDING & A JOB

We decided to make it a short engagement and chose September 9th, 2005 as our wedding day. The fast-approaching day also became a self-imposed deadline to do something about my flagging career.

I didn't want to start married life with casual work as a barman as my only source of income. I wanted to contribute towards buying a house and raising a family so I had to find a better job.

Everyone else I knew seemed to be forging careers and moving forward. For me, it seemed there was a big, black hole in my CV and it was getting bigger.

Prospective employers wanted to know why I only spent a few months working with Deutsche B.A. and why there was a year missing afterwards. They didn't want to know any more once the issue of critical illness was raised.

There was a confidence problem too because I had none. I felt incapable of handling any responsibility or stress. I hesitated to respond to job vacancies where before, I would have rushed off an application.

My training as an accounting technician was coming to an end but I needed work experience to pass the course.

Finding employment wasn't proving easy as my confidence was at an all-time low. I applied to many advertised vacancies without any success so Edel encouraged me to knock on doors and cold-call to find work. I hated doing it. I had absolutely no self-esteem, and it seemed, trudging around with a CV, that I was getting rejection after rejection.

I knocked on the doors of accountants' offices like Ernest & Young and KPMG and called to the accountancy departments of companies like Dunnes Stores and Penneys.

It was only on an off chance that I went to Merlin Park University Hospital in Galway and dropped my CV into the personnel office there.

I'd almost lost hope of finding a placement and completing the course when I received an unexpected phone call from the hospital's payroll manager, Sean Molloy. He was hiring two people to help set up the now infamous PPARS health payroll and personnel system.

Sean explained that he only had funding for two weeks. He asked if I wanted one of the positions. I leapt at the chance. I had nothing to lose except two shifts a week as a barman.

I started work in the hospital's accountancy department in January 2005 just eight months before our wedding. Just as my fledgling two-week career in accounts drew to a close, we got word that the government increased funding for my job by another month.

I was about to clear my desk at the end of that month when a woman in the general accounts department went on maternity leave, and the HSE offered me nine months more employment. Just as the new mum was returning, someone else left on long-term sick leave, and I was asked to stand in for him. And that's how it went on for years.

It wasn't ideal. I was on casual contracts with the HSE, so I was always looking over my shoulder expecting to be told I was surplus to requirements. Instead, thankfully, I went from department to department without any break in employment.

A few months after starting my new job, I received notice of my annual check-up and MRI scan in Beaumont Hospital in Dublin.

In the years since the surgery in 2000, I often feared that the brain tumour was returning. My stomach lurched every time I had a headache or double vision, but the MRI scans came up clear every time.

The doctors reassured me there was nothing there to worry about, but nothing would assuage the anxiety.

In 2002, in particular, I didn't feel well but the medics said I was fine. It felt like déjà vu. The German doctors didn't recognise a problem when it was staring them in the face. Why should I have confidence that things were any different with the doctors in Ireland?

The constant anxiety made me depressed. I wasn't motivated to find work or even to get out of bed in the morning.

"What is the point of anything, when I'm going to be dead soon anyway?" I thought.

If I was able to drink, I might have turned to alcohol. Fortunately, however, after the operation in

2000, my body no longer tolerated alcohol for some reason. Even today I don't drink because, after even one or two pints, I'm floored.

And as the years passed without incidence, my confidence grew, and I started to feel less apprehensive about a potential recurrence. Finally, I accepted that my fears were all in my head and that I was cured.

By the time, the appointment arrived for my annual check-up scan in 2005, I nearly considered not going for the scan at all.

What was the point of going all the way up to Dublin to be told the same thing again? I only reconsidered because the check-up marked the 5th year since my initial diagnosis.

Five years is not a magic marker or a date when you can announce to the world that you're cured. But it's a nice round number, and it's seen as a significant milestone, so I kept the appointment.

I took the train to Heuston Station and caught the number 14 bus from the city centre to Beaumont. I think I was more concerned with making the 5.30pm train back to Galway that day than the results of the scan.

I had absolutely no symptoms, and no headaches so I never thought for a minute there would be a recurrence.

Confident of getting a clean bill of health from the consultant neurosurgeon, Mr David Allcutt, I breezed into his office for the results.

"Hi David! Hope everything is well with you these days?"

A spry man with slightly receding hair, David didn't return my smile as he usually would.

"I'm sorry John, we've a bit of bad news," he said.

I stared at him in shock. This couldn't be happening, not now, not with our wedding around the corner.

"I'm afraid the tumour is back again."

Fear twisted in my gut, and I started to tremble.

"The scan shows that it's growing at the site of the original tumour. The good news is that it appears to be contained in that spot, but you're going to need surgery."

The news chilled me to the core, but my first thoughts were about the wedding. Would I be alive to make it?

Or if I survived the surgery, what condition would I be in? I knew from my experience in Germany that the recovery could be long and complicated.

"I'm getting married in September, can I delay the operation until after the wedding?" I asked.

I tried to control that note of rising hysteria in my voice.

"Well, you need to go home and speak to your fiancée, but we wouldn't recommend that you delay this too long. You need this surgery sooner rather than later," he replied.

I stumbled out of the place in shock. My hands shook as I tried to phone Edel but there was no answer.

She replied after I dialled her the second time but I could hear a tone of annoyance in her voice.

The hospital appointment hadn't weighed heavily on either of our minds, and she had forgotten about it.

"What do you want? I was in a meeting!"

She was irritated, but I was furious; furious at my body; at fate; at life in general.

"I have a f****** brain tumour!" I yelled.

Afterwards, I stood dazed at the bus stop as I made my way back to Heuston Station. It felt surreal to see life go on as normal while my world crashed down around me.

My mind raced as I considered the surgery. The timing was all wrong. There was too much potential for things to go awry. What if I didn't recover in time for the wedding?

I couldn't let Edel marry me with brain surgery hanging over us. What if things went drastically wrong?

I didn't want her stuck with someone who might end up in a nursing home for life. All those things went through my head.

Edel and Fergal drove to Athlone to meet me and by the time I got off the train, I'd made the decision to go ahead with the operation before the wedding.

"I'm going to have the surgery and I'm going to be well enough to get married in September," I said with a lot more confidence than I felt. The prospect of having another surgery on my brain was, frankly, terrifying.

"We'll stick to the plan until we can't," added Edel, coining a phrase that was to become a mantra in our lives in the years that followed.

The unfairness of it all hit me, and I was angry for a while. But there was nothing I could do about it except put my life in the hands of the surgeons again.

The day before the surgery, I was admitted into the Adams McConnell neurology ward in Beaumont Hospital. The ward couldn't have been bleaker. All the other patients were critically ill and only semi-conscious at best. It was a reminder that I didn't need about the seriousness of a brain illness.

The 2005 UEFA Champions League final between Liverpool and Milan took place that night in May. Friends of mine, who are big Liverpool fans, flew out to the now legendary match known as the Miracle of Istanbul.

The favourites, Milan, were 3-0 up by half-time and many Liverpool fans started leaving the Ataturk Stadium in disgust.

Lying in the darkened ward, I could hear excited roars coming from the TV room down the corridor. Liverpool had launched its comeback and scored three equalising goals during the second half.

Still lying in the hospital bed later, I heard shouts of joy as Liverpool won the penalty shoot-out 3-2.

The jubilant cries made me feel even more alone and sorrier for myself. All I wanted was to be a normal person, living a normal life, and preoccupied with something normal like a football match.

Everyone else seemed to be carrying on with their lives. Yet here I was lying in a hospital bed, in a ward full of misery with the threat of death or permanent disability hanging over me. I hardly slept throughout that long, dark night.

The surgery took six hours, and I was pretty sick afterwards but felt thankful that there was no paralysis, no speech defects or any of the long-term side effects that I'd experienced before.

There were, however, unexpected complications during the surgery.

"We discovered seven smaller nodules of tumours that didn't show up in the MRI," explained Dr Allcutt afterwards.

"We're confident that we've removed all trace of the tumours. But because the tumour was a recurrence, and because we found other nodules, we're scheduling radiation as a precaution."

I was happy to take any course of action that might prevent this happening again.

"Just as long as I can still get married in September," I said.

It was around this time that the 'C' word was raised for the first time, and the term 'cancer' became interchangeable with 'tumour'.

Up until the date of the recurrence, I was certainly under the impression that the tumour was benign. I know now that any tumour in the head can kill you, so there's no such thing as a 'benign' one. But the word 'cancer' adds another level of danger and fear to the word 'tumour'.

Six weeks of daily radiation began that summer in a new radiology clinic in Galway University Hospital.

The treatments were due to end on Friday, September 9th, our wedding day. However, the radiation therapist scheduled a double dose on Thursday 8th, to keep the wedding on course.

I was fortunate to be working for a state body like the HSE rather than a private employer. I was only new in the job and on contract, but they gave me time off work for the surgery.

As I'd also scheduled time off for our wedding, I made sure to work all through the radiation treatments.

We shelved plans for a honeymoon in exotic Dubai, as I couldn't fly for months after surgery. Instead, we booked a stay at the Inchydoney Island Lodge resort in Clonakilty in Cork instead.

As the wedding got closer, however, my mother worried that Edel hadn't thought things through.

"You know, the lad has nothing; he has no money, no career, he's very sick," she said. "Are you sure you know what you're doing?"

Edel was clear about what she was letting herself in for. We laid all our cards on the table. Despite everything, she was still determined to marry me, which says more about her than me.

Thankfully her parents, Michael and Josephine Tobin, didn't have any second thoughts about the wedding either. They've always been more than welcoming, and I get on really well with both my in-laws.

To be honest, I had little involvement with the organisation of the wedding. Edel said if I handled the tumour, she'd handle the wedding preparations. So all I had to do was show up in Edel's hometown of Cashel on September 9th.

Edel stayed with her parents for the week of the wedding while I had to remain in Galway for the treatment. She felt very lonely that week and I felt left out of things. I missed a lot of the run up to the wedding so it wasn't ideal.

On the positive side, Edel didn't get uptight about any of the usual disasters that befall the best of wedding preparations. In our circumstances, the little things didn't really matter.

"Whatever, it'll be fine!" was Edel's motto that week.

I finished radiation with a double dose as scheduled the day before the wedding and drove straight to the rehearsals.

Radiation is extremely tiring, but I was on a high at the thought of getting married. I also felt like a bit of a Superman to finish radiation one day and get married the next.

Nothing is going to beat me, I thought. Nothing is going to stop me marrying Edel.

In reality, I wasn't well. I was underweight and sick, and Edel was worried about me. The lower back of my head was bald from the radiation, so I was resigned to a bad hair day for our wedding too.

Missing the All-Ireland hurling final between Cork and Galway the day after our big day weighed on my mind too.

It's rare that I'd miss any Galway hurling or football match never mind when they're in an All-Ireland final. Edel urged me to go to the game, but I had the sense to realise that I'd only get married once, and there would be other Galway matches.

I arrived in Cashel just in time to preside over the catastrophe of the wedding suits. They'd been hired in Galway, and everyone waited until I arrived to try them on.

Legs were too short; legs were too long, and I think legs were even missing in the trousers. The arses were ripped, the flies were broken, and the jackets were all the wrong sizes. Edel's poor mother was up half the night fixing the suits on everyone.

I spent my last night as a single man with my family in a rented house outside the town. I woke at 5.00am and went out for a walk to clear my head. It had blazed sunshine all week in Tipperary, but a misty rain was starting to fall that morning.

I couldn't believe this day was actually happening and that, at last, I was getting married. There was no sense of having cold feet, just overwhelming excitement and anticipation of it all.

My groomsman Fergal, the man who introduced me to Edel, came out into the garden that morning, and he laughed, and I panicked as we wrote the groom's speech together.

As we left for the Church of St. John The Baptist for the 1.30pm ceremony in the town, it was spilling rain. After a week-long heatwave, monsoon season had arrived in Cashel. As I darted from the car to the church, a hunched figure stretched out a bony hand and grabbed me by the arm.

"It's a sign of good luck when it's raining on your wedding day!" the woman assured me from under her rain hat.

We should have had lots of good luck so, because the rain bucketed down all day.

I took my position in front of the altar with my brother and best man, Padraic, as we waited for Edel to arrive.

My heart was drumming loudly in my chest, and my anxiety levels rose by the minute. I shifted uncomfortably in my seat and tried to loosen my collar.

Padraic grinned and nodded towards an exit door to the right of the altar.

"Go for it, John, it's your last chance!" he said.

The seriousness of what I was about to do had hit me as soon as I stepped inside the church.

I wondered if I would be around for Edel, if I'd be able to support her and if I would be everything she hoped I'd be. I had all these doubts running through my head.

I was afraid, I'm still afraid, that I might let her down by dying. My thoughts were quickly interrupted because Edel arrived right on the appointed hour for the wedding.

She was at the church door and suddenly, there was no going back. This wedding was really happening.

It wasn't any surprise to me that Edel made a breathtakingly beautiful bride. Carrying a bouquet of Calla Lilies, she wore an ivory halter-neck gown with a delicate sprinkle of beads that sparkled in the dim light of the chapel. A full-length veil with a train trailed in her wake. Her sister, Marie, and my twin, Cathy, were her bridesmaids.

Edel was a vision coming down the aisle, but she was a blurred one as my eyes filled with tears.

My father-in-law was supposed to hand over his daughter at the end of the aisle. Then, as rehearsed, Edel and I were to proceed on to the altar together. Instead, father and daughter forgot to stop and passed me by beaming broadly. I had to run up to the altar after them.

Once I had Edel standing beside me, all my fears fell away, and a sense of calm took their place.

The emotion and the enormity of the day, however, stayed with me. I'd survived another surgery; I'd finished radiation, and now I'd made it to the altar to marry my soulmate.

I felt grateful to be there. I could hardly repeat my vows I was so choked up. In fact, I shed a lot more tears than Edel did during the proceedings.

Edel's late uncle, Fr Martin Ryan, came out of retirement to perform the wedding ceremony. We were very fond of him and he was always a huge support to us whenever times were tough. He was a man who was very knowledgeable and well-read, but he wore his intellect lightly. He was happy to talk about Shellac nails with teenagers, about hurling with me, and the finer points of existentialism with university dons. He could relate to everyone on a personal level.

Edel's sister Marie, who's a gifted musician, offered to play the violin at the wedding. But Edel was concerned because she only took up playing the violin a year before we married. When she heard Marie practising, she thought it sounded off-key and screechy.

Each time she went to her mother's, she'd ask: "Is she getting any better?"

Her mother wasn't reassuring. "No, but she's practising so much, you have to let her play anyway!"

Marie went on to perform Eileen Iver's hauntingly beautiful piece, Bygone Days, with aplomb.

In fact, all of Edel's family performed during the ceremony. Edel's brother James played the organ and her other sisters, Bríd and Joan, played the cello and tin whistle. Even my songbird bride took part in the ceremony to sing Taste and See (the Goodness of the Lord) from Psalm 34.

Fr Martin was a bit out of practice by the time he officiated at our wedding so he forgot to announce us as husband and wife.

This resulted in some confusion. I never got to kiss the bride; the congregation never got to clap and at one stage Edel whispered to me: "Are we married, now?" The ceremony ended with a fizzle rather than a bang.

Fr Martin was so upset and was kicking himself afterwards. We had to reassure him for ages after that hardly anyone noticed and that we didn't care.

And we didn't care. It was the little unexpected things and all the chaos that made the day more memorable.

The driving rain ensured that no one lingered outside our country church wedding. Nor did they stop off into any of the pubs between the church and the Cashel Palace Hotel where we held our reception.

We hired a pianist to tinkle the ivories in the hotel foyer, but so many people flooded in at once, that she was drowned out in minutes.

We also had a sparkling wine reception, but the place was drunk dry within the hour.

The Cashel Palace Hotel was a grand old Georgian mansion hotel that in its heyday hosted legends like Jackie Kennedy, Elizabeth Taylor and Richard Burton. It had acres of beautiful blossoming gardens where we planned to take all our wedding photos, but we never stepped outside the door with the weather.

It didn't matter to me. The rain couldn't dampen my spirits that day. I was on a massive high from the sheer excitement of the wedding and the exhilaration of marrying Edel. I felt on top of the world now that we were embarking on a whole new chapter in our lives.

Of course, exhaustion hit me like a sledgehammer in the following days. All the happiness and optimism faded along with my energy.

The doctors said the tumours were gone, but they'd said that before. The fact that the last MRI missed several tumours concerned me too.

All I wanted was the chance of a life with Edel, but neither of us was as confident as we used to be that we'd have the happy-ever-after ending.

There was a black cloud following us around again, and we had to keep looking over our shoulder to see how close it was.

From now on life would be laced with fear and uncertainty. We fought off this dangerous intruder twice, but we knew now it could come back and attack at any time.

OH BABY!

While a family was always something Edel and I wanted, we decided not to rush into it after getting married. I was still suffering from the after-effects of the brain tumour and we felt that we weren't financially or emotionally ready to start a family straight away.

But by 2008, we agreed that we were as ready as we'd ever be and having a baby topped our 'to do' list. Back then we still naively thought we could plan our lives. Edel used to have 'five-year plans' and having a baby went to the top of our plan that year.

We were excited and full of anticipation. We were young and feeling healthy, and both of us thought we'd have a baby in no time.

So when nothing happened immediately, Edel began to get concerned. While I preferred to stick my head in the sand, Edel was proactive about things as usual.

With the help of Dr Google, she learned that prolonged medical treatments including radiation could affect fertility.

"Do you remember anyone telling you this before any of your treatments?" she asked.

"I think I'd remember it if someone mentioned anything like that," I said. "It's not the kind of thing you're likely to forget, is it?

I was always full sure that we'd have children so I was shaken to the core to think that it might not happen for us.

I think I was even more upset for Edel. After everything I'd been through and everything I'd put her through the least she deserved was the child that she wanted.

Given my medical history, we were quickly referred to the Galway Fertility Clinic, and we faced a battery of tests with growing dread.

"The results are generally positive," said the doctor. "Some aspects are sub-optimal and this is likely to have been caused by John's medical treatment. But overall, it's good. There's no cause for real concern."

"Isn't it great to get some good news from doctors for a change?" I said.

Edel wasn't quite so optimistic even though the doctor said we shouldn't rule out a natural pregnancy. He recommended IUI or intrauterine insemination to start.

When several rounds of IUI didn't work, we were advised that we might need more advanced technology to achieve our dream of having children.

Our tests showed we were suitable candidates for ICSI, a form of IVF or In vitro fertilisation. It's a procedure where they inject sperm into the egg before implantation.

After more tests, our first round of ICSI was lined up for early 2010.

The cost of the treatment was going to be a huge financial burden, particularly at a time when we were trying to buy a new house. But like most people in that situation, having a baby took precedence over everything else.

I'll confess that in the beginning, I saw fertility treatment as a terrible failure on my part. Fertility and virility are closely associated in the male psyche, and I definitely felt my masculinity was being called into question. Once again my body was letting me down.

Perhaps naively, given my medical history, I'd never dreamed we'd have any problem getting pregnant. But here we were resorting to technology, doctors and clinics and Edel was undergoing dangerous and highly intrusive procedures.

I just felt emasculated and embarrassed by it all. I hated even having to walk in the door of the fertility clinic.

During my second or third visit, I sat there with my head in my hands in the waiting room one day. I was feeling humiliated and more than a bit sorry for myself when a guy from my old school walked into the clinic.

This wasn't just any guy; he was the most handsome guy who ever attended our school or possibly any school in Ireland ever.

He was tall, well built and unreasonably good-looking. The girls fawned over him and the guys wanted to be him. If Angelina Jolie had clapped eyes on him, Brad Pitt would have been dumped.

Mr Universe and I looked at each other, nodded and exchanged grim but knowing smiles. It sounds stupid but from then on I never worried about going to the clinic.

I figured if infertility can happen to the best looking and most macho guy in Ireland, it can happen to anyone.

It actually helps to be macho when you're doing IVF. We discovered, like many others, that it's an incredibly stressful procedure and not for the faint-hearted.

Even after everything we've been through with my medical issues, if you asked us the hardest thing we faced, we'd both say IVF.

It was a time full of heartbreak, tension and raw emotion. It's not a time in my life that I recall with any affection.

The one thing that provided a welcome distraction during this period was a horse called Operation Houdini.

This bay gelding came into our lives a couple of years earlier when my Uncle Gabriel asked if I knew any guys who'd be interested in forming a racing syndicate.

He said he knew a trainer called Davie Fitzgerald who had a young horse and he looked promising. It sounded like fun so a group of about 10 friends and colleagues all chipped in €1,500 to buy a bit of a leg each.

He was christened Operation Houdini in memory of a night and a student that I knew years earlier.

It was college rag week and everyone was going partying except us because we were stony broke. This guy came up with the brainwave of going around the entire college campus asking people if they could loan him 20p to use the phone box.

The ruse was so successful that he raised enough money for both of us to go drinking that night.

"That was a narrow escape," he said as we laughed in the pub later. "I think we should call the ploy, Operation Houdini!"

Our equine version of Operation Houdini turned out to be a fine earner too. The horse won five races, came second eight times, and earned €140,000 in prize money during his brief four-year career.

It was during the time when Edel and I started undergoing fertility treatment that he won the Munster Grand National in Mallow by a nose in November 2008.

Several of us in the consortium were at the track and we roared, screamed and hugged each other and ran to the winners' enclosure. Our elation was cut short by the announcement of a stewards' enquiry.

It emerged that the runner-up complained our horse had crossed his path six furlongs from home. None of us, including the jockey, could believe that the complaint was even entertained. Ten minutes later, the runner-up, was awarded the race.

The winners' purse which was worth Sterling £23,000 was snatched from us and instead we received second prize of Sterling £7,000.

Operation Houdini went on to run in the Midlands Grand National and the Welsh Grand National in 2009. He even ran in two Irish Grand Nationals in Fairyhouse in 2009 and 2010 but fell in both of them.

The horse paid own way and gave us a lot of great days out. He came second in his final race at Cork Racecourse on October 31, 2010.

Shortly after, he was diagnosed with rheumatoid arthritis in his right foreleg. We tried to get him fixed up but they had to put him down at just 9 years of age.

My heart was never in racing again after that and any buzz that I got from the racetrack went forever.

In the months leading up to Operation Houdini's ultimate demise, Edel and I were still concentrating on fertility treatment and doing everything we could to improve our chances of having a baby.

We consulted with alternative health therapist who provided us with nutritional advice. I ate nuts like a squirrel and stuck rigidly to the diet and followed all the advice.

We were walking, exercising, eating super foods and doing all the things that might boost our chances of success. I was feeling super healthy, really virtuous and highly stressed.

Edel was having the crazy mood swings associated with the hormone injections for ICSI.

At this stage we were ground down by four failed IUI treatments, a failed ICSI cycle and we were embarking on a fresh ICSI cycle again.

One summer evening, when I badly needed to get out of the house, I went for a game of tennis with a friend, James O'Carroll. Mid way through the game I felt a hot, piercing pain down through my left leg and calf.

We were playing the best of 13 games and I wasn't about to throw in the towel so I fought on. The game finished at last.

"Jesus, I need to sit down," I said, collapsing on the court. "I'm in total agony with my leg"

"What is it, cramp?"

"I've no idea but I won't be going anywhere for a while."

James offered to drop me home, but I finally mustered up the courage to get back on my feet and hobble to the car before driving the three miles home to Barna.

The pain got worse as the night went on and I had to sleep on the floor that night to get any relief.

The next morning, a colleague, Taryn saw me drag myself into the office.

"Jesus, John, what have you done to your leg?"

"I've no idea – I got this terrible pain while I was playing tennis last night and it's still killing me."

"It's probably your sciatic nerve," she said, "You need to see a good physio."

I was relieved when another colleague, Orla, knew a physiotherapist who agreed to see me straight away. I drove to his practice but I couldn't even get onto his massage table. I can't describe the pain, it was that bad.

He managed to lower the table and lever me up, but when he touched my back, I nearly leapt off the table again.

"You need to see your GP right away," he said. "I can't do anything for you at the moment".

My regular GP is Dr Adrian Carney at Roscam Medical Centre, but Dr Susan Kennelly saw me at short notice that day.

"I can't tell what's going on, John," she said "I'm going to refer you to the Bon Secours for an MRI. I'll see if they'll take you straight away."

I drove from the doctors' surgery and had the MRI in the Bon Secours. I never thought for a moment the pain was anything more than nerve damage or a pulled muscle from the tennis match.

Dr Kennelly said she'd let me know the results as soon as she got them but it would take a few days.

Two days later, Edel was still a hormonal mess and I was still in severe pain and hadn't slept properly in days. It was a Friday of the June bank holiday weekend and we were both frazzled.

Edel had to go into work so I decided to head for the peace of the countryside and my parents' house. There was no one there when I arrived but just then, Dr Kennelly called.

"John, I've just got the results of your MRI," she said. "I'm sorry to tell you but its shows a large mass of tumour in your lower back."

I closed my eyes and thought, "Oh no, here we go again." The monster from the black had reared its ugly head and struck again.

"The tumour is compressing the spinal cord and is causing the pain you're experiencing," she explained.

A tumour; I had another bloody tumour and this time on the spine. I thought of Edel and the state she was in. God, this was all she needed to hear.

"I've been trying to get in contact with Beaumont Hospital to get you in straight away," Dr Kennelly explained. "But with the bank holiday weekend, it's impossible to contact anyone."

She said she would keep trying but she'd definitely get an appointment after the weekend.

"I'm on my way to Cork for a family event," she added. "But if you need anything, anything at all, just call my mobile".

Shocked and dazed, I wandered towards the stables where my sister, Laura, was working. She was the first to hear the news.

I didn't even want to tell Edel but in the end I phoned her at work and let her know. After a shocked silence, she said she'd be straight down.

Mam and Dad returned then. They didn't show any visible alarm, which, suggested they might have suspected the worst all along.

113

As the shock wore off, I began to feel more positive. I'd done this twice before, and at least I had an explanation for the pain this time. I'd just have treatment again and get better again.

"Don't worry" I assured Edel "We've gone through worse before. It's just a small setback. I can handle this".

We all went to a local restaurant called Finn's for dinner that evening. Neighbours who I hadn't seen in a while started coming over for a chat.

"Howaya John, how are you feeling now?"

"I'm grand, couldn't be better! I replied even though I could hardly sit down or eat with the pain. It felt like it was getting worse by the hour.

Even amid another cancer crisis, we resolved to keep to the schedule for making a baby. 'We'll stick to the plan until we can't,' was the mantra and we returned home to Barna so Edel could take her hormone injections.

The pain was intolerable when I tried to lie down. I was so sleep deprived, that I nodded off for a few hours sitting upright.

I woke up in agonising pain about 1.00am and tried to distract myself by watching TV.

We were both required in the fertility clinic the next morning. It was another vital part of the cycle and after all the hormonal treatment Edel had been through, I didn't want to be the one to jeopardise the whole procedure.

By now I'd learned fertility treatment involved multiple steps all choreographed with the precision of a Swiss watch. I had to make sure I was available for my small bit.

I planned to make it to the clinic first thing in the morning, do what I had to do and then go straight to A&E.

In the early hours of the morning, however, I could no longer handle the burning pain licking up my back. I started looking at my phone and wondering if it was too early to call Susan Kennelly.

I managed not to call until 5.00am and then I couldn't take the torture anymore. I didn't expect her to answer the dial tone but she did.

"Susan, I'm so sorry for calling you at this hour but I just can't cope with the pain anymore."

Even though I'd woken her, she knew what to do.

"OK, get Edel to take you to A&E," she said. "I'll let them know you're on the way."

Edel managed to get me into the car and to A&E where I got the morphine injections and the relief I desperately needed. They told me I was going to be transferred to Beaumont Hospital for surgery once a consultant signed me off.

I made room for Edel on my hospital trolley and we lay there under the flickering fluorescent lights. We were both mentally and physically exhausted. Both of us were required at the clinic but I never felt less like making a baby in my entire life.

"Let's forget about the ICSI, we need to focus on getting you better," she said.

We continued to lie in silence for a few minutes. But then we began thinking aloud about what treatment might lie ahead in Beaumont Hospital.

What if it permanently affected my fertility this time? What if this was my last chance to have a child?

The hours from 5.00am dragged on, and there was no sign of my transfer to Beaumont happening. We decided Edel should meet our appointment at the clinic, 10 minutes away. She could update them on my condition and ask for their advice.

Less than an hour later, Edel arrived back carrying a sample pot and a consent form. The clinic's advice was to collect a sample and freeze it for the option of future use.

Unfortunately, there was another hurdle. It was a bank holiday, and no embryologist was working in the clinic that day.

A fertility nurse called Emma doggedly tracked down the only embryologist left in Galway. Fiona gave up her day off to help us and to this day, we owe her our gratitude. Now I just had to do my bit.

"Can you ask a nurse to find a wheelchair for me?" I said.

"Are you sure you're able to do this?"

"I'm not doing much else hanging around here am I? I'll give it a go!"

We'll draw a veil over the subsequent events but somehow I managed to hand over a specimen jar with the vital baby-making ingredients.

Edel made the dash to the clinic two miles away and our chances of a baby were preserved for the future.

When I think back and remember how close we were to abandoning the treatment that day, it terrifies me.

Our first daughter, Fírinne and later our son Ríain were conceived as a result of our efforts that day. I'm eternally grateful that we stuck to the plan.

Despite arriving at dawn, I was still waiting 12 hours later for a consultant to sign me off for a transfer to Beaumont.

The bank holiday was presenting serious problems for the Registrar and he was getting increasingly concerned as my symptoms worsened.

The pressure on my spinal cord was now severe and they feared it was only a matter of time before I could lose vital functions.

Yet he couldn't find a consultant to assess me and sign my transfer papers. The delay was becoming worrying.

A panicked Edel approached the doctor.

"Should John just discharge himself so I can drive him straight to Beaumont?" she asked.

"No, that might incur delays when you get to Beaumont," he said. "They'd have to start the admission process from scratch. I'm also concerned about problems developing during the journey. The risks are too high."

So we waited; me in increasing pain and Edel in increasing fear.

A consultant finally showed up to scribble a signature on the transfer form, and another shot of morphine was approved. An ambulance whisked me to Beaumont while Edel and my sister, Alma, followed in their car.

High on morphine, the trip was a brief blur. I remember the flashing blue light and the siren and wittering to the paramedic, and suddenly we were at the hospital.

Edel and Alma reached the hospital shortly after me. Edel's heart sank when she was immediately directed down a hospital corridor without even asking for me.

She needn't have worried. The morphine had sent my motor mouth into overdrive, and the entire hospital floor heard me broadcast that my fabulous wife Edel and my wonderful sister Alma, were on their way.

A weary Texan doctor was assessing me when Edel found me. I was busy listing everyone I ever heard of in Texas and every other United State of America to find out who we knew in common.

It was the early hours of the morning, and the exhausted doctor wasn't much in the form of being harangued by a highly medicated Galway man.

"OK, so you don't know Mickser Lally, you wouldn't by any chance know a guy called…."

This time I was under the care of neurosurgeon consultant David O'Brien who specialises in both brain and spinal surgery in Beaumont.

A fellow Galway man, I first met him in 2009 when he stepped in for Dr David Allcutt during an annual check-up.

It turned out he grew up five minutes from my home in Salthill. David is a compact man in his early fifties who boasts a good head of silver hair, a ready smile and lots of energy. He likes to high five his patients – I think he must have spent a lot of time training in America.

He's very approachable, and I'd always feel comfortable calling him and asking him questions. He often phones to see how things are going with me too.

He came to my bed with the consent forms and an MRI scan shortly before dawn. The drugs were wearing off, and I was a bit more alert. He explained his plans for the surgery and the tumour located in the lumbar spine.

"It's likely that this growth is from your brain tumour of 2005," he explained. "Cells from that tumour may have broken away and were carried to this new site in the fluid circulating your nervous system.

"We don't know how long this tumour has been growing there. Once it ran out of space and started pressing on the spinal cord, you began to feel pain.

"Once they start, the intensity increases quickly over a short period."

David has always been honest and never makes any false promises.

"John, I don't know if I'll be able to remove the full tumour," he said. "I won't really know what we're facing until we open you up and take a look".

He described how he would permanently remove a small part of my spine to get access to the tumour. Then he gave me the consent form that listed all the risks of the surgery. It wasn't pleasant reading.

He repeated everything I read just in case it wasn't crystal clear to both of us.

I'd have preferred not to know there was a significant chance that I might not walk again, could be rendered impotent or lose bladder or bowel functions.

Still, I assured Edel that I'd be all right as I kissed her goodbye. I felt more exhausted than I felt worried about the operation because I hadn't slept in four nights.

The operation took place a couple of hours after arriving in Beaumont and lasted about five hours. As soon as I was conscious, I was aware of feeling a lot better than I did before the operation.

Instead of a hellish burning pain down my back and leg, I only had a small ball of scorching fire in the small of my back. After reading the risks to the surgery, I was grateful that I could feel anything at all.

David said afterwards that he was confident he removed most of the tumour.

However, he couldn't gauge the success of the operation until I had another MRI scan after the surgery wound had healed.

"I removed as much as I could see," he said. "I took the pressure off the cord, and the pain will be gone as soon as the wound in your back heals."

He added; "It's a case of wait and see what needs to be done next."

Over the next few weeks, I was barely able to walk with the pain. There was an anxious wait of days before all the other functions highlighted on the 'risk list' returned to full working order.

Meanwhile, all around me, there were many bleak reminders of how insidious and dangerous brain tumours can be.

In the TV room, I met the mother of a patient from Wexford who was diagnosed with a brain tumour. She told me how her young daughter was admitted for surgery that week but upon opening her up, they discovered they could do nothing for her. The poor woman was reeling after her daughter was given a week or two to live.

I shared a ward with three other guys who all had brain tumours of one sort or another. One of them was a lovely man from Carlow in his mid-thirties whose wife and young children visited every day.

He had an inoperable brain tumour, but he was up and about and in good form. I was shaken to learn that he had died a week after I left the hospital.

Again, hospital was a wake-up call. Death became a depressingly real prospect, and I felt a real fear at that time. But it also served to remind me how lucky I was. I was still alive and feeling well.

It was a stark reminder to focus on the positive and to embrace all the good things in life.

So I couldn't have been happier when Mam had a brainstorm. The new tumour and continuing fertility treatments were wearing us all down.

"Right, I think we all need to get away," she said. "We're going on a holiday, and I think we should go to South Africa."

It was just the tonic we needed. Edel and I had a honeymoon of sorts in Dubai a year after our wedding when I recovered from treatment.

But we'd never gone travelling like we once had planned and South Africa beckoned to us like an exotic dream.

We sat down and researched the trip for weeks. We would fly to Cape Town and travel down the Garden Route and go on safari along the way.

In the middle of all this, we discovered, to our joy, that Edel was pregnant. Finally, things appeared to be going our way.

We were ecstatic, but we hardly dared let ourselves get too excited until Edel passed the first trimester. We decided to hug the secret to ourselves for a while.

Edel would be past the three-month mark by the time we went to South Africa so we continued with our holiday plans, went to the travel agents and booked everything.

Our holiday of a lifetime was set for January 2011, which would be mid-winter in Ireland and mid-summer in South Africa. We were having a baby and heading to paradise. It was all going to be so perfect.

FÍRINNE

The dream lasted exactly a week. A few days after we booked the holiday, I went for an MRI to mark three months since the spinal surgery in Beaumont.

It was October 2010 and David O'Brien phoned with the results a few days later.

He had never claimed that the tumour was gone, but he seemed happy after the surgery. They had totally removed the tumours in my previous two surgeries, so I thought this would be no different.

I felt really well. I was back at work and my dream holiday was less than ten tantalising weeks away. Being ever the optimist, I just assumed I was 'cured'. So his opener shocked me.

"John, I've bad news for you," he said.

No one jokes about these things, but I still replied: "You've got to be kidding me!"

"I've looked at the MRI, and as I suspected, I'm afraid I didn't get the entire tumour out," he said. "It's growing again, and it's going to cause you problems. We'll have to operate again."

We had this long conversation as I tried to negotiate an alternative to surgery but there wasn't one.

"I don't think you should hold off on this," he said. "You need to have the operation this side of Christmas."

It was the last thing I needed to hear. I'd dreaded telling the office that I needed more time off for another operation.

Just like our honeymoon, our grand plans for South Africa were gone up in smoke because I couldn't fly long haul for months after spinal surgery. The news was a low blow to all of us.

Instead of the holiday of a lifetime, I was back to gloomy waiting rooms, hospital wards and more surgery. That threatening black cloud hovered over us again.

The prospect of having a baby was the light at the end of a very dark tunnel. My focus turned to Edel and the baby. We didn't want to tempt fate by making plans for a baby but the idea of our first child kept our spirits buoyant. It kept us sane during that time.

Still, I don't think either of us exhaled until Edel had passed the three-month mark and the chances of a miscarriage decreased.

We were still fearful of what lay ahead for me but the pregnancy was a hugely positive thing in our lives now.

Edel, like me, is an optimist by nature and we soon relegated the impending surgery to a small setback in our lives. It was bad news but we could deal with it.

As soon as I had another operation, life would get back to normal, and we could look forward to our future.

Meanwhile, if Edel ever worried about the impending surgery, I'd brush it aside.

"Forget about the small stuff, I'll handle that," I said. "You concentrate on the big thing. The most important thing is we're going to have a baby next year!"

I don't remember much in the lead up to the hospital admission that December. I tried to remain optimistic, but deep down I was terrified at the prospect of another surgery and all its inherent risks. I just wanted to get it over with.

I was on the surgical schedule for 9.00am, Monday, December 13th but the operation could only go ahead if I could get a bed in Beaumont.

So we went through the bizarre and stressful routine that every patient goes through where you phone Beaumont after 3.00pm on the eve of your operation to see if you're getting a bed.

Every patient who calls this number is sick and anxious anyway. Many have to take time off work, arrange childcare and travel from the other side of the country. And all of the anxiety, organisation, and travel may be for nothing if there's no bed for you.

With no guarantee of a bed, Edel and I decided to drive half way up from Galway to Tyrellspass in Westmeath on the eve of my surgery.

We waited there until 3pm to call the hospital but the hospital told us to call back in an hour. They don't call you back; you have to call them and they may answer the phone but more often, they don't.

We called several times before they could confirm that a bed was available. We drove the rest of the way to Dublin and once again I found myself in a bed in the Richmond Ward in Beaumont.

As usual, David O'Brien came to see me before the operation. Using diagrams and scans, he explained all the complications involved in the surgery ahead. The tumour was now attached to vital nerves at the end of the spine known as cauda equina or 'horse's tail'.

As usual, the prognosis wasn't encouraging.

"Damage to these nerves can cause permanent paralysis, impotence, impaired bladder or bowel control or difficulty walking," he said. "So I'm going to take out as much of the tumour as possible while trying to avoid these nerves but again, it's still unlikely I will be able to take all of it out."

The surgery took around eight hours and this time I was in a bad way when I woke up. It was the second surgery in the same area so it was more complicated than the last one.

Once again, I woke with cannulas and drains coming out of my back and I needed a catheter to drain urine from my bladder. It also felt like they'd left a branding iron burning through my back. I was also in a world of pain and every movement was agonising even though I was on morphine.

To make matters worse, I knew that the tumour, or at least part of it, was still there anyway. I was still unwell when I was finally released on December 24.

The pain had been so severe that I couldn't eat and I'd lost a lot of weight. Gaunt and skeletal looking, I didn't recognise the caved-in face that looked back at me in the mirror. My bladder still wasn't working properly and the catheter had to stay in for six weeks at least. So to add to all the festive fun, I still had drains and bags and wires hanging off me.

Despite all the pre-surgical warnings, I was still shocked to hear that there was 50-50 chance that my bladder function would return at all.

I felt rotten and I looked haggard but at least, I reasoned, I was getting out of the hospital for Christmas.

While I was cocooned in the overheated environment of the hospital, the coldest winter in 130 years of met office records raged outside.

There were arctic conditions with blizzards, snowdrifts, and travel chaos across the country. Record low temperatures of -17 degrees Celsius were reported in parts of the country in that week.

My Dublin-based sister, Alma, and brother-in-law, Andrew Croghan, volunteered to get me to Galway on Christmas Eve. Thick snow blanketed the entire country and most roads were impassable but the route between Dublin and Galway had been cleared.

A journey that normally took two or three hours took more than six hours. Andrew had to drive in second gear most of the way to my parents' where Edel and I were spending Christmas. Mam came out to the car as we arrived.

"Sorry lads, we've no water," she said. "The pipes are frozen. The plumber is here and he's trying to heat the pipes to unblock them."

Our local plumber is a guy who was couple of years behind me at school.

I was carrying my catheter bag and drains and I was wearing a tracksuit and feeling tired and cranky after six hours in the car. The last thing I wanted was to socialise with an old school pal.

I crept to the back door in the hope of hobbling up the stairs and out of sight. Of course, he walked straight out the back door as I was going in.

"John, great to see you and Happy Christmas!" he said not batting an eyelid and as he went on about his business. He could see that I was in no condition to chat about the football results.

I was the Grinch who stole Christmas that year. Contrary and ill-tempered, I didn't want to talk to anyone or meet anyone. I was fed up of looking at four walls but I couldn't get back to work until they removed the catheter. The dream holiday to South Africa in the New Year was scrapped too and I blamed myself.

The only positive was that Edel was pregnant but I felt so sick and miserable that even the prospect of a baby couldn't lift my mood.

It didn't improve in January either when the urologist said he still couldn't remove the catheter because nothing happened when he did.

Over the next two weeks, they tried removing it five times but nothing happened and I still couldn't urinate on my own.

I was terrified at the prospect of forever having a catheter bag attached. My head spun when they brought me to a meeting where they discussed how they would insert a permanent one.

I refused to resign myself to that future. They saw that I was adamant and agreed to let me try having the catheter removed again.

My stomach was churning as I told the nurse in the urology department that this could be my last chance. She saw my despairing face and came up with a new plan of action. She brought out a huge plastic bottle and filled it with water.

"Go for a walk around the hospital and try to drink all of this. Then come back to me and let's see what happens," she instructed.

I did exactly as she said and even though I feared buckling under the performance pressure, this time the catheter removal was a huge success.

Who'd have guessed the pure joy that I'd get one day from having a pee? It was like winning the lotto all over again.

The HSE's Occupational Health Department assessed me and declared me fit for work again.

After 43 days of hospitals, surgery, waiting rooms and hanging around the house, I got back to life in the real world on January 25, 2011.

Of course, I knew more treatment lay ahead. David O'Brien said that both chemo and radiation would be necessary to keep the tumour on my spine in check.

But the bad news just kept on coming. After the next scan, I learned that the original tumour on the base of my back had company. Two new growths had suddenly appeared further up my spine.

The hospital decided I needed to go ahead with treatment of 28 days radiation with six weeks of chemo administered through an IV drip.

We talked through the treatment options with my radiation oncologist, Frank Sullivan, at University Hospital Galway at the end of May.

"Edel is due in a few weeks. I don't want to be sick and in the middle of chemo and radiation when the baby arrives," I said.

Frank was reassuring.

"Don't worry, John, we can delay things a few weeks to give you all a chance to enjoy the new arrival. You're doing well and you've no symptoms."

Of course, within days of Frank's words, I started feeling symptoms with a twinge here and an ache there. I didn't say anything to Edel but as the days passed,. I knew the tumour was growing and would cause real problems soon.

I made an appointment with Frank again and he confirmed that even though the baby was on the way, we couldn't delay treatment any longer. He would try to get me into the schedule as soon as he could.

Meanwhile, Edel sailed through her pregnancy avoiding hazards like morning sickness and swollen ankles.

Her maternity leave started early July and she began 'nesting' as people call it. The term doesn't really do justice to someone who turns into a cleaning maniac and reorganises the entire house.

I was in work on Monday morning, July 4, when she rang.

"I was lifting the telly and I felt something go 'pop'," she said.

Our television was the big, hulking type that took two men to move.

"What were you doing lifting the telly?" I almost shrieked. "I'll be home in a minute to get you straight to the hospital!"

I got her to the University Hospital Galway where she was seen almost straight away. While we were with the doctor, the friendly face of a lady from Campbell Catering appeared around the door.

"Hi ya love!" she said to Edel. "Will you have the beef or salmon for your dinner?"

"Thanks anyway, but I'm not staying!" replied Edel.

That's when the doctor announced: "Order your dinner, you're staying all right. This baby is on the way."

We both looked at each other in shock.

A few hours later, I was ambushed again. My phone rang and I stepped outside the labour ward to take the call. It was the radiation department in the same hospital.

They had found a slot in the schedule for treatment planning. They wanted to apply radiation tattoos that they use as a bullseye target for the treatment.

They're made using a drop of ink and a slender needle. I've a great collection of radiation tattoos at this stage.

"We want you to come in now if you can," said the radiologist. "Can you make it to the hospital in the next 20 minutes?"

"I'm here already. I'm in the labour ward with my wife."

I thought Edel seemed to be handling things extremely well because, so far, there was none of that screaming that I'd seen on the telly. I told them I'd be there in a minute.

"Don't worry, we'll whisk you in and out in no time," assured the radiologist.

I told Edel that I was just going out for some air. As I walked across the hospital, I thought about the possibility that I'd be in the radiation department of the same hospital at the same time that my first child was being born.

After the appointment, I dashed back breathless to Edel's bedside. She was worried because I was gone for so long. I was on steroids at this stage and was prone to a bit of drug-induced erratic behaviour. Edel told me later that she feared I wasn't coming back.

The labour was fraught or at least it was for me.

"Don't panic, John, just don't panic," I kept telling myself. "Just hold her hand and keep breathing."

I scanned the midwives' faces to try and gauge their reaction to the unfolding carnage. I took my cue from them, and as long as they weren't screaming and panicking, I guessed that I shouldn't either.

It was shortly before midnight on July 4, 2011, American Independence Day, that our beautiful child emerged.

She had an audience of doctors, midwives and interested parties including Edel and me.

Our little russet-faced baby looked suspiciously to the left at one doctor, then to the right to look at another, and then the child looked straight at me and howled.

"It's a girl!" said the midwife.

"What's she on about?" I thought to myself.

From where I was standing, which was somewhere between Edel's head and the exit, the new arrival had all the accoutrements of a boy.

I was 100% sure that it was a boy but I was outnumbered by an army of busy women so I didn't feel in any position to argue. They'd laugh at their mistake later.

They asked me if I wanted to cut the cord but I couldn't think of anything more terrifying.

After all Edel and I had been through to have this child, I couldn't risk maiming her. I didn't even want to hold her in case I'd drop her.

"No!" I said. "You're the professionals, please you do it!"

They handed over our first little bundle of light and joy and I saw they were right about her being a girl. She was a healthy 7lbs 4 oz.

We called her Fírinne, which was a name that Edel heard a few years earlier and remembered because she thought it was so beautiful.

The name is the Irish word for 'truth', which also resonated with Edel.

I loved the name too but after everything Edel had been through, if she wanted to call our daughter 'Pocahontas', I'd have been perfectly happy.

RAGING BULL

Take it from me, that radiation, chemo and a new-born baby are an exhausting combination.

Of course, the timing of my illness and treatments was impeccable. I'd been waiting for years for this baby. But the first day we brought her home from the hospital, I had to leave and head back to the hospital to start chemo.

Those early months turned out to be a bittersweet experience. I wanted this baby so much but in the early weeks, I was in too much pain to even physically hold her in my arms. I was feeling exhausted and, at the same time, frustrated that I couldn't fully enjoy my time with her.

Radiation is tiring and it's monotonous going to the hospital every day, week after week. However, it's a doddle compared to the weekly chemo treatments, which, are long and very unpleasant.

In my case, I was expected to arrive at the hospital at 8.30am. The nurses chat away as they check your blood pressure and heart rate and get you seated into the Buxton reclining chair. Then the oncologist or oncology nurse checks everything before inserting the IV and hooking you up to your first infusion.

You start out chatting to other people around you, but then the treatment starts making everyone drowsy and the room gets quieter and quieter as the hours pass.

I find it difficult because I hate to have to sit still for so long.

The caterers serving tea or the nurses changing the infusions are the only break in the dreariness. The morning and afternoon tends to pass in a blur and finally, around 4.30pm, it's all over.

Even if you enter the hospital bright-eyed and rosy cheeked, your complexion is grey and you feel like a zombie by the time you're finished.

When Fírinne was about three weeks old and I was about three weeks into the treatments, the nerve pain in my back became unbearable.

They say it's a sign that treatment is working but that's not much comfort when you're in agony. I was due for another chemo session the next morning but I didn't feel like going ahead with it.

The hospital decided to prescribe higher doses of steroids called Dexamethasone, which reduce inflammation and relieve the pressure on the spinal cord. The pain ebbed away to more bearable levels.

Unfortunately, there are less positive side effects to high dose steroids and in my case, they dramatically alter my mood and behaviour.

Edel says she can even see my physical appearance change once I'm on steroids. She sees a strange glaze appear in my eyes and there's always an odd sheen to my skin when I'm taking them.

But the worst thing for her is that I behave like Jekyll and Hyde when I'm on these drugs. Even though they get the pain under control, I lose control of my mind.

After Fírinne was born, my head was racing all the time and I hadn't the attention span to look after a baby. I couldn't sit still for an instant and I couldn't sleep and I was constantly ravenous. I had to be fed more often than the baby.

Edel couldn't leave me in the house with Fírinne for any length of time. I was liable to walk out and forget that the baby was there. So even when Edel went to the shop, she had to bring Fírinne with her.

Leaving the house with a new-born is as complicated as a military expedition, so Edel tried to limit her excursions by bulk-buying the shopping for the week.

Her plan didn't work. With my steroid-fuelled appetite, I gorged everything in the house within days and she'd have to pack Fírinne up and head to the supermarket again.

I remember one day at my in-laws' house, Edel looked on in horror as I ate twelve potatoes with my dinner. I only stopped at twelve because there were no more left.

And if Edel wasn't feeling insecure enough as a first-time mother, I was inadvertently doing my best to help her feel even worse.

She was forced to listen to me telling her that she wasn't feeding Fírinne right or that she wasn't bathing her right. To be especially helpful, I wrote up lots of 'To Do' lists for Edel too during that time.

She'd be up several times at night with the baby and then would arrive downstairs in the morning to see me waiting with a list of chores that she simply had to do that day.

Once she learned it was pointless arguing with a crazy man, she'd take the list.

"I'll get right on it," she'd say although it was usually said in a tone of voice that I didn't appreciate.

The truth is that Edel could have easily coped with being a first time mother except she had a bigger, and far less sweet-natured, baby to deal with at the same time. She had to do everything for Fírinne because I was no help at all.

Edel also had no chance to have post-natal depression because I had first dibs on all the mood swings and temper tantrums in our house. You couldn't look sideways at me without an argument breaking out.

She despaired because there was no reasoning with the rage-filled beast she lived with.

"John, you're not talking rationally. It's the drugs. You need to calm down."

But I'd blow a fuse at any suggestion that the drugs were affecting me.

"What are you talking about? There's nothing the matter with me. I'm not behaving rationally? I'm the only sane one around here. This place is a complete mad house. Jesus, I have to get out of here before I lose my mind!"

Cue the front door slamming.

Then I'd stomp off for a twenty-mile hike from one end of the city to the other. I'd be fuming all the way even though I couldn't tell you what the argument was about in the first place.

Luckily, throughout all this, Fírinne was the perfect baby. It was as if she knew there was something amiss because she was the most easy-going new-born ever. It's safe to say, the early months of our first baby weren't the idyllic time we'd hoped for, but it certainly wasn't Fírinne's fault.

At last, the chemo and radiation came to an end and so too did the steroids. The incredibly angry hulk vanished and we resumed some semblance of normal life again.

I got back to work in September 2011 and also knuckled down to the business of buying a house for our family.

Before we married, we bought a house in Tuam. We were 22 miles from Galway city and Edel would have preferred something closer to the city.

However, property prices nearer the city were soaring and our capacity to borrow from the banks was also restricted because I was unable to get life insurance for a mortgage.

I loved our first house in Tuam. It was just 8 miles from my parents' in Liskeavy and close to the town where I went to school so I was completely at home there. The house was spacious, bright and modern. We were happy there for more than three years.

But Edel grew tired of the long commute in traffic to work so we decided to sell up in 2008. It turned out to be a stroke of luck because we were one of the last houses to sell at boom prices before the property bubble burst. The house sold before we managed to buy another place, so we ended up renting a place in Barna closer to the city.

We didn't mean to stay there for long but, with my medical concerns and, what felt like relentless IVF treatment, we ended up living there for nearly three years.

After renting all that time, viewing houses became an obsession for me. I must have looked at around 60 properties. It was a frustrating search because despite scouring all the websites and looking in all the areas we liked, I saw nothing that grabbed my interest.

Then one day after Fírinne was born, I was looking through DAFT and I spotted a three-storey, art deco style house in Salthill that was new to the market. It was quirky, a little unusual; I liked the look of it.

"Take a look at this," I said showing it to Edel on my laptop. "This house looks a bit different."

Edel was intrigued too, so that day we drove to Salthill to see what it looked like from the outside.

The paint on the windows and doors was blistered and peeling and the woodwork underneath appeared rotten. The glass was dark and grimy and the garden was overgrown.

The house looked rundown and unloved and we immediately fell for it.

It was a semi-detached house built in the 1930s that was an executor sale and had lain empty for some time. It needed complete renovation inside and out.

My uncle-in-law, Jimmy Kelly, is a building contractor so he priced the job for us.

On the positive side, he told us that it was structurally intact and had a good roof. We loved that there were fireplaces in every room and that it was full of original features and odd cubbyholes.

We also learned that turning the house into a comfortable family home would involve a lot of demolition, a lot of rebuilding and a lot of money.

Property prices were rock bottom at the time but the renovations were set to cost us as much again as the house. Still, we decided that we loved the property enough to throw in everything we had, and more.

The contracts on the house went through two days before Christmas, 2011 and my uncle and his crew began working on it in the New Year.

By now, I was symptom free and pain free and my energy levels after the chemo and radiation were returning. I looked and felt OK and it almost seemed like the previous year was a distant nightmare.

An MRI in the New Year confirmed everything was well. The tumour hadn't grown and there were no recurrences in the brain. Finally my health had stabilised and I could take a breath and reflect on everything.

It was around this time, I first began to consider getting a second opinion on my treatment.

I felt grateful that I had come so far, that I was feeling good, and was still largely unscathed. But I didn't want a repeat of the last year where I was operated on twice, treated with aggressive radiation and chemo and yet still hadn't got rid of the tumour.

I also knew if this tumour on the spine started to grow again, I could be in big trouble. My neurosurgeon in Beaumont, David O'Brien, had indicated that any further surgery in the area would be high risk especially after radiation. I knew too that I had a narrow escape from nerve damage to the bladder from the last surgery.

Yet, more radiation was not an option. That area had already been irradiated and the spinal cord was unlikely to tolerate more.

Hoping that there might be other options or treatments out there, I thought it might be time to get a second opinion in the U.S. or elsewhere.

I tentatively raised the subject with Frank Sullivan, Professor of Radiation Oncology, at Galway University Hospital during an appointment.

Frank's name keeps coming up in my treatment. He's been in charge of my case since I started receiving radiation in 2005 and he has become like a brother to me.

A large, twinkle-eyed man in his mid-fifties, he has a great head of grey hair, a beard, and a ready smile and he's always there to offer good advice.

Still, I hesitated about asking him for a second opinion. I didn't want to seem ungrateful and offend him and the other professionals whose skills had kept me alive.

Still I felt I owed it to myself and to my family to explore every option out there. I just didn't know how to begin. It turned out I was over-thinking the situation because Frank was completely supportive.

"I think it's a great idea," he said. "If you were anyone in my family, I'd encourage you to look at all the options and seek a second opinion too."

He referred me to one of his colleagues, Catherine Copertino, who's a director of a cancer institute in Maryland in America.

She advised that the best hospital for cancer treatment and research is the Memorial Sloan Kettering Cancer Centre in New York. Liaising with her, I had my medical files sent to New York.

A neuro-oncologist called Thomas Kaley, who specialises in brain tumours in Sloan Kettering, looked at my case. Unable to resist the opportunity of dealing with a rare liponeurocytoma, he agreed to a consult and I received an appointment to see him in New York in January 2012.

We decided to take advantage of the appointment to turn the trip into a weeklong family holiday to New York. Edel, Fírinne and my mother, Carmel, all travelled to the Big Apple too.

Fírinne was born on American Independence Day six months earlier so I thought it was appropriate that her first holiday was to the U.S. Her christening, coincidentally, took place on another red-letter American date which was 9/11 or September 11.

We flew to New York from Shannon and stayed for a week in The Park Central Hotel on 7th Avenue. It's located across the road from the iconic Carnegie Hall and a few blocks away from Central Park. It was also close to Sloan Kettering and, more importantly, for Edel and my mother, close to Macy's department store.

New York was freezing cold and we were all exhausted because Fírinne's body clock was all over the place. She was wide-awake by 5.00am, so I'd end up walking the hotel with her to ensure the shoppers got their beauty sleep.

Fírinne was enchanted with the hotel doorman, a towering black man, who must have been seven-foot tall. He'd swoop down into her little face and he'd boom in his broad Noo Yawk accent: 'How's mah liddle sweedhard this morning?" She'd respond by gurgling, shrieking and clapping with delight.

My mother was more enchanted with Macy's especially as they offered a 10% discount because she was 60 and another discount because it was a blue moon or something.

We went to the Statue of Liberty and Ellis Island and we did the horse-drawn carriage ride in Central Park and all the touristy things you do in Manhattan. Even though I enjoyed it, I couldn't relax until I had the consultation at Sloan Kettering.

On the day of the appointment, my mother baby-sat Fírinne while Edel accompanied me to the consultation rooms at Sloan Kettering. We complain about the cost of consultants here but this single consult cost over $3,500. I was determined to get there well before the appointed time so I wouldn't miss a second of it.

After entering the lobby of 205, East 64th Street New York, we were directed to a lift that would bring us to Dr Kaley's 'suite'.

His 'suite' consisted of consulting rooms and a reception area in the middle of a spacious and plush waiting area filled with comfortable couches.

The receptionist waved airily towards an array of drinks and a buffet of cold snacks that we could avail of while waiting for our appointment.

"Is this a hotel or a hospital?" I asked Edel.

After a brief wait, Dr Kaley, emerged to greet us and bring us to his office. He was younger than I expected. Bald, bespectacled but with a round, fresh face, he may have been in his late 40s.

My files were on his desk and from our conversation, it was apparent that he had looked through them all.

He was reassuring in that he said the treatment that I received in Irish hospitals was on a par with anything they were doing in America.

"After reviewing your whole case history, I can say that there's nothing that we would have done any differently here," he said. "You've been receiving the best and most up-to-date treatments for your condition."

Sloan Kettering is renowned for its cutting-edge research and he also offered an option if there was a recurrence of the tumour.

"We have a trial for a new chemotherapy drug that we'd be willing to offer you if your tumour starts growing again any time soon," he said. "But for the moment, I can't see that we can do anything more than what's being done in Ireland."

Edel and I left the hospital feeling that the trip had been a positive one. We had been reassured that my treatment programme was correct and we had been offered a new treatment option if the tumour returned.

Afterwards, I discovered other medics in Sloan Kettering Hospital had reviewed my medical files. Among them was an oncologist in Beaumont called Dr Patrick Morris who went on a fellowship to Sloan Kettering a year after my appointment.

"You don't know me but I know all about you from Sloan Kettering," he said. "I remember reading about your tumour. I didn't know I'd be getting the chance to meet you in person!"

After returning home reassured from New York, we hurled ourselves into the renovations of our first proper family house.

Every day at lunchtime, I looked forward to going to the site to see the builders' progress.

Initially, the house was filled with the rubble of its old parting walls and looked like a derelict ruin. Then gradually, it returned to its art deco glory days.

Edel designed all the interiors and we added on a new extension to transform the property into a modern family home. We moved into our dream home on June 28th that year.

While our house was still undergoing a major transformation, I decided it was time for a personal one. I made up my mind to head back to college but this time, I was determined to graduate.

There was a recruitment moratorium in the HSE then so there were no new job postings available. Nevertheless, I thought it would be no harm to upskill myself.

I didn't know what course I wanted to do until I came across a course in Addiction Studies in The University of Limerick. I never knew such a field of study existed until then, but I knew straight away that it was the course for me.

I'd missed the closing date for applications, but I pleaded my case to the head of the course and explained that I worked for the HSE and The Child and Family Agency.

A lot of service users with the agency have experienced addiction in their lives or are addicts themselves. I'm not employed specifically as a counsellor, but I felt the course would still be helpful in my work.

If I managed to complete the course, I'd gain the practical skills to respond appropriately to service users with addiction problems.

The course was intense because it took place 7.00pm to 10.00pm every Tuesday and Thursday with an additional full day of classes every second Saturday for a year.

It also entailed a three-hour round journey to the University of Limerick after work twice a week so it was a big commitment.

As I hadn't been in college for 12 years, I found it quite daunting. My classmates were clinical psychiatric nurses, counsellors, members of the guards, social workers, and professionals working with addiction in their day-to-day work.

It helped that I loved the subject matter. I also got great help in my end of year project thanks to the former governor of Mountjoy, John Lonergan.

I met John when he was invited to give a talk during a training day that the child and family department holds a few times a year.

After 42 years in the prison service, 24 of them as them as the most senior prison officer in the country, he knows all about disadvantaged children and families. John's a captivating speaker who gave a passionate and inspiring talk on family systems.

I thought he might have useful statistics for my project, which was about the link between socio-economics and addiction. So I introduced myself after his talk and asked him if he could provide any information on addiction in prisons.

I remember John laughing as he replied: "This is going to be a long conversation!"

He said he wouldn't be able to give me all the facts and figures in a five-minute chat but, in his professional opinion, he believed that 95% of prisoners have addiction problems or issues of addiction in the family

"I tell you what, I'll take your number, and I'll give you a ring tonight," he said. "I'll phone you around 6.30pm."

I was thinking to myself, 'you will all right.' I assumed I was getting the brush off.

"OK, fantastic!" I said.

I left thinking that would be the last I heard from John Lonergan

But at 6.30pm, the phone rang. John stayed on the phone until about 8.30pm that night, filling me in on everything I needed for my project. He gave me was two hours of solid facts and information that I'd never have been able to access without his help.

It was also impressive to have facts, figures and insights on addiction that were all attributable to the foremost authority on the Irish prison system. So it happened that John Lonergan featured large in my project and my grade.

Afterwards, I read with interest about another talk that he gave where he insisted that prison is the worst thing that can happen to you after ill health.

"If someone gave me a choice tomorrow morning of a very serious illness, like cancer, and treatment in the Mater Hospital, or five years in Mountjoy, I'd opt for five years in Mountjoy," he said. "Why? Because I'd say 'I'll come out of Mountjoy. I'll survive it, and I have my health and in five years' time, I'll be back again on my feet.' I mightn't survive the Mater Hospital and serious cancer or any other serious health disease. So I'm just saying you have to put prison into perspective. I'd hold onto my health first, and after that, I'd say the worst experience for any human being is to be sent to prison."

I was amazed by how much he thought about it. I always thought long-term illness is like a sentence. And I have to agree with him. If I had the choice, I'd do five years in Mountjoy too.

I'm proud to say I completed my degree in addiction studies. I never had the greatest levels of concentration so it required hard work to keep up. It helped that I had a great project and great material for it thanks to John.

In the end, I finished in the top three of the class, which I was thrilled about. For me, it was a great achievement. In fact, completing the course and graduating was one of my proudest moments. It ranks up there, just below marrying Edel and having children.

FATHERHOOD & RÍAIN

The arrival of our second child, Ríain is proof that anything worthwhile in life takes effort and hard work.

Both Edel and I wanted Fírinne to have a brother or sister but we'd been through a lot the first time. I didn't dare hope that we'd be lucky enough to have another baby.

A big part of me felt it would be tempting fate to wish for any more, but Edel was determined to at least try. So towards the end of spring 2012, we went back to the clinic.

Once again, it wasn't an easy process, and we went through a number of failed cycles. By October, we accepted that maybe it wasn't going to happen for us again. We were beginning to think that it was time to move on with our lives and be happy with the little miracle we had. We agreed to try one last time.

Nothing seemed to go right with this treatment cycle. I heard phrases like 'poor hormonal response', 'poor fertilisation rates' and 'slow embryonic growth.'

We resigned ourselves to the fact that this cycle wasn't working either. Then, against all the odds, Ríain was conceived, and we were the happiest couple alive.

From early on, Edel had an idea that the baby was a boy because he was so energetic. You're supposed to be able to detect babies' sleep patterns from their behaviour in the womb so it didn't augur well when

Edel said: "This child never seems to sleep!" He appeared to be on the go, day and night, even in the womb.

The nine months were drama free ones, and everything went smoothly. We didn't know that it was the calm before the storm.

As our little girl, Fírinne was such an easy-going child, I'd have been happy if we had another girl. While either sex would have been fine, I suspected that maybe a boy wouldn't be as easy to handle and boy, was I proved right there.

But as soon as Ríain was born in the early hours of Saturday morning, August 31st, 2013, I was thrilled to be told we had a boy. I pictured me and my little sidekick in the years ahead decked out in our Galway jerseys heading for Croke Park.

Once again I left the cutting of the cord bit to the professionals. Scissors in the sweaty hands of a shaking layman, in a delivery room, is an accident waiting to happen.

I've always reasoned that each of our babies is so precious that there's no point in taking chances.

There was no chance of Ríain getting mixed up with any other baby in the hospital. He was born with such a huge mop of spiky black hair that it distinguished him from every other new-born in the country.

"Wow, he has a great head of hair!" exclaimed one of the nurses. "That's amazing! I wonder if he'll lose it all, though, they often do."

But he didn't. Instead, his hair began to get thicker and longer, and his first visit to the barber was at the age of three months.

The first time I became a dad, I was apprehensive, but I was positively smug about fatherhood the second time around. After Fírinne, I believed parenthood was easy. This was no problem; Edel and I had this whole baby thing worked out. We were baby-raising experts; veterans in the field. The truth was we hadn't a clue what was about to hit us.

From the moment he was born, Ríain refused to give us a night's sleep. He survived on catnaps and never developed any sleep pattern. He fought against every single bedtime.

As soon as we had him settled, he'd wake again, fists clenched and bellowing for attention. Our lives were turned upside down. We became prisoners in our home, as he wouldn't go in the car or travel anywhere without screaming the entire way.

It felt like Ríain cried all night, every night but he just never slept. When there was no prospect of sleep, I'd put him in his buggy at around 3.00am and walk him down the prom in Salthill. That way, at least Edel and Fírinne got an hour or two of sleep.

The combination of the motion, the sound of the sea crashing on the stony beach and the cool night air would finally lull him to sleep. I'd sleepwalk back to the house.

I'd only crawl back into bed when his cries would ring through the house again. Stumbling up again, I'd put him in the buggy and stagger back down to the promenade to pace until dawn.

We were mentally and physically exhausted, and our happy household became the land of the living dead. Chronically sleep deprived by an insomniac new-born, an energetic tot and the demands of two jobs, we were walking zombies.

To cap it all, I was aware that I was starting to feel unwell again. There was a vague but undeniable feeling of pain down one of my legs that was developing into a limp.

We tried everything with Ríain. We brought him to his GP who diagnosed reflux, a condition where acid in the stomach comes up the gullet and causes a burning sensation. The reflux medication helped settle him but only slightly. We tried changing his milk, but that didn't help matters at all.

In desperation, we brought him to a cranial osteopath. They use massage techniques on the skull to release stress and pressure in a baby's head and neck. It worked for a week or two and then we were back to square one again.

The only consolation throughout it all was that he was a thriving baby. He wasn't losing weight, and he wasn't sick.

However, Edel and I were constantly at the end of our tether and went around with bloodshot eyes and suffering from crippling tiredness.

My mother used to smile knowingly to herself whenever we complained. The non-sleeping and the constant hyperactivity was history repeating itself. It turns out Ríain is a mini-me.

"It's exactly what I had to go through with you," she'd say.

Edel insists that all the sleeplessness stopped before Ríain's first birthday, but I recall that it went on like this for at least two years. Or maybe it just felt like that.

Then for no apparent reason, the 24-hour restlessness all just stopped. There came a night when we gave him a bottle, put him down and he slept until morning without waking. That became the new normal.

Ríain was completely different to Fírinne in every way. Even now as a toddler, he's a larger-than-life character. Everything is 'big' with Ríain. He's all big hearty laughs, hot sobbing tears and huge, passionate bear hugs. He's always in a big hurry and when he's cross about anything, everyone knows about it.

As a baby, he was a nightmare to bathe or clean; he hated water. With so much hair, it had to be shampooed and blow-dried from the time he was born. Maybe it was as a result of this, that he developed a visceral hatred for baths and any activity linked to hygiene.

Even a nappy change was a battle of wits. He was like a wriggling Houdini when you wanted to wipe him down or clean him up. There was no mistaking that this was a boy.

To this day, bribery remains the only thing to persuade him to get into the bath. We've tried everything else and failed dismally.

Our hopes were raised recently when an episode of his favourite cartoon character, Peppa Pig, featured bath time.

"Peppa loves the bath. Friday is Peppa's bath day," ran the commentary.

Grabbing my chance, I asked, "And what day is your bath day, Ríain? Is it Friday?"

Edel and I could only laugh when he turned, looked me in the eye and replied with dead certainty: "It's over!"

Our first nine months with our third baby Saorla is a huge contrast to Ríain's first year. Saorla is an incredibly easy baby. She's a placid, constantly smiling child who only cries when she wants to be fed or needs a nappy change. Once that's fixed, she's back to smiling again.

She's a magical baby; a little pixie with dancing blue eyes, an infectious smile and a tinkling giggle. Being in a bad mood around Saorla is impossible.

However, Ríain wasn't cheered by the arrival of a new baby sister when we first brought her home. He looked at her and said: "Aaaah, baby!"

Then he turned to Edel and said: "She's tired. Put her in her cot upstairs now."

Fírinne had a similar 'take him or leave him' attitude to the arrival of baby Ríain. She just appeared bored by his presence. As the years have gone on, that's changed, and now they can't do anything without each other.

Even though there are two years between them, they're the A-Team now. They can play together for three hours one day and then the next day they'll spend three hours fighting.

But when Fírinne walks into a room now, the first thing she has to know is 'Where's Ríain?' and he's the same.

Ríain must have absorbed a lot of life during his long waking hours as a baby because he's the creative one when it comes to role play. Fírinne joins in his games of 'pretend' rather than the other way around.

He decides that he's a superhero one day or the ice-cream man the next. He instructs Fírinne on her role in his fantasy land and then he narrates an entire story for the pair to follow.

He's also mesmerised by tractors, lorries, diggers, and cars or anything with a motor. We saw him peddling his little motor trike with our sweeping brush stuck into the front last week. When we asked what he was doing, he informed us he was the road sweeper.

Just turned three-years-old, he has no interest in sports yet, but when he throws a ball, he aims it straight. He's left-footed and left-handed, but when he kicks a ball, he kicks with power and direction. He has deadly accuracy, which gives me great hope that he'll play for the Galway team someday!

He decided to rename himself over a year ago and announced that he forthwith wished to be known only as Boo.

So he was called Boo until recently when he wailed: 'Stop calling me Boo, my name is Ríain!' We all had to revert to his real name which is still an adjustment as we all got used to him being Boo.

Fírinne's pet name since she's been a baby is Turtle or Turts. I was reading one of those waterproof books when she was in the bath and telling her: 'here's a fish' and 'look at the seal' and 'here's the turtle'. She had only started to babble 'Mama' and 'Dada' when all of a sudden she looked up at me with her big eyes and yelled 'Turtle!' It was her first time to repeat a word.

Ríain proved my earlier suspicions that boys are a lot more hard work than girls in the beginning. Yet he's now growing into a sweet, happy-go-lucky child. His internal clock is still a bit messed up sometimes. He arrived in on top of us at 3.26am this week. I know the time; I squinted at the clock.

"Daddy!" he said as he flung his arms around me. "Aren't you my best friend?"

He was still chattering away in the dark about SpongeBob SquarePants by the time I fell back asleep. Mostly, though, Ríain is an easy-going child. You can talk to him, reason with him and give him a toy car and he's in ecstasy.

Fírinne is another story entirely. They say boys will wreck your house but girls will wreck your head, and I believe it now. Fírinne is age five going on 25. She's morphed into a princess who reigns with an iron fist and a wrist full of pink bracelets.

"Did you get me a present?" is a familiar refrain.

"Fírinne, you got a present last week."

She never skips a beat.

"Yes, Daddy, but I need a present THIS week."

Even a couple of years ago, Fírinne had everything worked out.

I tried to put her to sleep after reading her usual three stories one night, but she threw her arms around my neck and put me in a headlock.

"Daddy, let's have a chat," she said.

"What do you want to chat about?"

"What will we do tomorrow?"

"Turts, that depends on what kind of a day it is

"Could we go to Loughwell Pet Farm?"

"We could if it's not raining but it was raining all day today."

She mulled over this for a few seconds.

"Yes, Daddy but you can go downstairs, turn on the telly and check the castfore."

It took me a few seconds before I realised she was telling me to check the weather forecast.

Another time, a midget-sized Fírinne started whining after I splashed on aftershave.

"Daddy, I want some!"

"Aftershave is only for grown-ups, not for children."

"But I'm a big girl," she argued.

"It's only for men, not for girls," I countered.

She paused for a second before screaming: "I want to be a man! I want to be a man!"

I roared laughing at the outburst.

Fírinne and me at my graduation from the University of Limerick,
the day before Ríain's birth.

Me with happy handfuls, Ríain and Fírinne, February 2015.

Daddy's Girl: Padraic, Fírinne and me at the All-Ireland semi final, Croke Park, Aug. 2015.

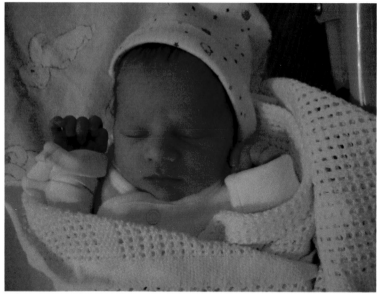

Miracle baby: New-born Saorla weighing in at just over 6lb.

Saorla's christening, March 2016.

Another milestone: Fírinne's first day at school. Sept. 2016.

Family portrait: August 2016. *(Photographer: Michael Reidy.)*

The A-Team: Fírinne and Ríain, August 2016 *(Photographer: Michael Reidy .)*

Baby blue eyes: Edel and Saorla, August 2016. *(Photographer: Michael Reidy.)*

Me with the radiation team at University Hospital Galway, August 2016.
(photo by Ross Cullen)

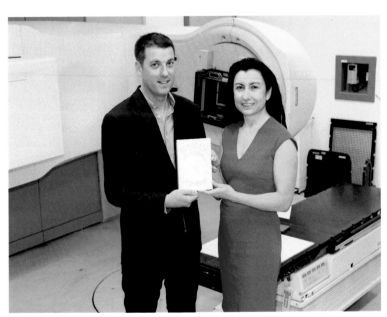

Me with Dr Anna Marie O'Connell, Consultant Radiologist at UHG.
August 2016. *(photo by Ross Cullen)*

Me with Professor Frank Sullivan at Galway Clinic, August 2016. *(photo by Ross Cullen)*

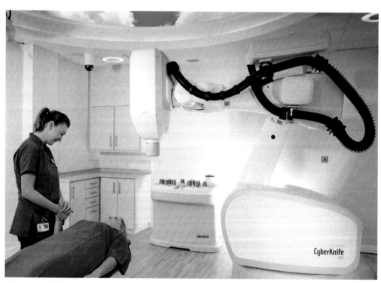

The CyberKnife machine that's keeping me alive and mobile. Hermitage
Medical Clinic. *(photo courtesy of the Hermitage Medical Clinic, Lucan Dublin).*

Fírinne glowered for a few seconds but then she laughed too.

"That was so funny, Dad," she said.

I was minding the kids just a few days ago and learned to my cost that her latest obsession is chewing gum. Her mother warned her that she's not allowed gum, but she figured out long ago that Daddy is made of less stern stuff.

"Daddy, can I have a chewing gum?"

"No, we've no chewing gum."

"Will you go to the shop and get me some, please?"

"No, you're not allowed have chewing gum."

"Please Daddy, please? Please, can I have it? Please, please, please…"

The authorities at Guantanamo could learn a few things from Fírinne. After a full hour of relentless pleading, threats and promises, I broke down and gave in. I went down to the local shop with her, got a packet of gum and gave her half a stick.

She popped the gum in her mouth, but before she even started chewing, she fixed me with a stern eye.

"Don't tell Mammy!" she said.

I love being around all three of them but it's not always easy when you're feeling below par. The worst time for me to be around the kids is when I have to use steroids.

Steroids have evil side effects and change your entire way of thinking and your behaviour. Even when I know I'm behaving out of character, I can't seem to stop it. I end up shouting and roaring, and I'm liable to erupt over nothing.

Then Fírinne sneaks up behind me and says she's sorry for something that she never did, and I feel like a total monster.

Even as a toddler, Ríain, could see that something was awry with me the first time he saw me on steroids.

"Daddy's a BIG bit cross today," he told Edel one day.

Steroid treatment is hard for everyone so I stay off them until I have no choice. Then when I feel that I'm turning from Jekyll to Hyde and my head is about to explode, I just disappear for a few hours and cool off.

Most of the time, I'm just as involved as Edel in raising our kids. I love being around them. They're a great source of positive energy but at the same time, they're exhausting.

Our schedule feels mental at times. When people ask if I watched some programme on TV, I try to explain that I've barely had time for a shower since Fírinne was born.

I feel constantly tired, dazed and addled, and I sometimes wonder if it's a side effect of my illness or if it's just from having three children under five.

All I know for sure is that I'm relieved when I realise that it's nearly 8.00pm because that's the kids' bedtime. I'm only fit for bed myself at that stage.

At the same time, Edel says that there was a fundamental change in me as soon as we had kids.

Parenthood changes everyone but in my case, the children have given me a new focus.

They have taken the spotlight off my health issues. They're a great distraction and a great focus at the same time.

The day Fírinne was born, and I was about to start another round of chemo and radiation, I remember wishing that I'd live to see her first birthday. Then when I got to her first birthday, I wanted to see her second one.

This year my focus was on Fírinne starting school in September and now that I've achieved that goal, I'd like to focus on reaching her First Communion. Fírinne is my marker for all the children's big life milestones. My goal now is to stick around and share as many of them as I can.

When our parish priest, Fr Gerry Jennings, christened Saorla this year, he said a dad sees his daughter in a white dress three times. After her christening, the next white dress is her First Communion, and then it's her wedding. I'd love to be around for Saorla's wedding, but I fear that's a milestone too far after all the medical interventions of the last two years.

There are times when I'm going through treatment, and feeling unwell, that I despair of not seeing their next birthday. Then there are times, like last week, when I get a good result after a scan, and I'm more hopeful about spending more time with my kids. It's a case of "Great, no new tumours! I'll live for another while yet!"

At the same time, every birthday or major event, I find myself wondering if I'll be around for the next one. I don't spend every happy family event anticipating my impending doom. I always live in hope, but I have to face the possibility that I won't see my three children reach adulthood.

That thought is always at the back of my mind, and it's also at the back of Edel's. The reality that I might not be around this time next year can have a positive effect on our lives too. It helps Edel and I focus on the present and to enjoy the moment.

We don't think or worry about anything too far ahead anymore; we live one day at a time and make the most of each day. Every day I can still get out of the bed, go to work and get the kids to crèche or school is another great day for me.

Meanwhile, the children are still too small to understand or to notice that their dad is sometimes unwell. The routine of life goes on, and Edel and I maintain a sense of normality in the house as much as possible.

Ultimately, my aim for Fírinne, Ríain and Saorla is for them to be happy and to help them form lasting and happy memories of their father.

If something happens to me, I don't want to be just a shadowy figure in their past. I want them to know who I am. I feel I've achieved that goal with Fírinne and Ríain to some extent, and I hope for the same with Saorla now.

In 20 years' time, if I'm not around, I want her to be able to say: "I remember my dad." That's one of my primary objectives for the children now.

Edel and the kids are what keep me going, and they're the reason that I never give up. But if the time comes that I can't be with them anymore, I just want them to remember me and to know how much they were loved.

CYBERKNIFE & SURGERY

It was summer 2014 and Ríain was less than a year old when I started to become aware of a slight pain my left leg. Hoping that it would go away and that it was just a pulled muscle, I tried to ignore it.

At the back of my mind, I knew it was something more serious. Sure enough, it developed into a limp, and the pain increased to the extent that I couldn't ignore it anymore. I turned to my usual stalwart, Frank Sullivan, at Galway University Hospital for help.

I always turn to Frank because I trust him, and I hate going the surgical route. At this stage, I don't want any more operations. The recovery time is much greater for surgery than it is for radiation or chemo.

As much as the doctors and nurses are great, I hate being in hospital. I'd have radiation and chemo any day before I'd have surgery.

Frank wasn't too surprised when I presented with these symptoms.

"I was expecting that tumour in your spine to start causing more problems at some stage," he said. "There are also some new spots further up your spine which we will need to watch."

"Spots," I thought. "That's probably not a big deal."

Because of his involvement in cancer research, he's familiar with the best medical technology. Frank suggested that I get assessed for suitability for a new and revolutionary treatment called CyberKnife.

However, he said he wouldn't decide on a particular course of treatment until the medical experts investigated every avenue.

"You can't rule out surgery if it's the best option," he said.

Edel and I knew a third surgery on the same part of the spine was going to be high risk especially after radiation. Any other option had to be better. We asked him more about CyberKnife.

"CyberKnife is only available in Ireland very recently," he explained. "It's a very high-tech alternative to conventional radiation or surgery. It's about high doses of radiation delivered to tumours with extreme accuracy."

He added: "As a non-surgical option, it might offer the best solution. It's often suitable for patients with inoperable or surgically complex tumours."

I was relieved when a couple of weeks later, David O'Brien, my neurosurgeon in Beaumont Hospital, agreed that CyberKnife was the best treatment option.

While conventional radiation blasts the whole area where a tumour is located, CyberKnife is a laser that's aims only at the tumour and shoots much higher doses of radiation straight into the growth.

X-ray cameras are used at the same time to monitor the position of the tumour and the movement of the patient.

Because it's so targeted, it limits the damage to healthy tissue around it. It really is revolutionary. It's especially useful for difficult tumours like mine on the spine, but it can treat growths anywhere in the body, including the prostate, lung, brain, liver, pancreas and kidney.

The CyberKnife system became widely available in America and the rest of the world around 2010. At the moment it's available in many hospitals in the UK, France, Italy and Germany. It was only around 2014 that it became available in Ireland, and only in the private Hermitage Clinic in Dublin.

It remains the only hospital in the country with the facility, which means not everyone can avail of it.

While waiting for the treatment at the Hermitage, the tumour grew, and the pain travelled to my hip as well as down both sides of my leg.

It was compressing the nerves in the spinal cord, and I was in agony. I refused to get into a wheelchair, but I was fit for one because moving around was excruciating. When it got really bad, the liquid morphine painkiller, Oramorph, was the only thing that provided relief.

After weeks of trying to avoid steroids, I had to cave and start taking them to alleviate the pressure on the nerves. Both Edel and I knew the next few weeks weren't going to be easy. Dr Jekyll and Mr Hyde were moving back in.

The effect of the drugs was as bad as ever. With the usual side-effects of insomnia and massive mood swings, I was bad-tempered and cantankerous, and I was no help with the kids.

Fírinne, who had become my little shadow since the arrival of her brother Ríain a year earlier, began to slink back to Edel's side. While still only three-years-old, she could tell her Daddy wasn't who he normally was.

Edel tried to keep a sense of normality, but life became easier for us all when I finally left for the treatment in Dublin.

Treatment began on Monday, September 8th, under the care of Dr Jamsari Khalid who also worked in University Hospital Galway. As CyberKnife was still new technology in 2014, I was only the 30th patient or so in Ireland to have the treatment.

Edel was working and looking after the kids, so my mother came with me to Dublin. We were able to stay in the Clarion Hotel next to the Hermitage because the treatment is performed on an outpatient basis and I didn't want to be in hospital for a moment more than I had to be.

Most patients experience minimal side effects and recovery time is instant apart from the tiredness.

The treatment is carried out in a windowless room in the CyberKnife Centre. It's all so high-tech that there's no need for a hospital gown. You can wear everyday jeans and sweater or even a three-piece suit if you prefer.

The pain was stabbing, and I could barely manoeuvre myself onto the table. Then it got worse as nurses tried to position me into place. In the end, I had to take the morphine to be able to get my spine flat for the treatment.

As soon as they arranged me to their satisfaction, the medical staff left, and I was on my own. Four or five cameras focussed on me while the team watched me on a screen in another room. They pipe music into the room to relax you.

"Are you feeling OK, John?" a disembodied voice asked.

"I'm flying thanks!"

I wasn't flying. The grinding pain in my leg was making it tough to stay still, but I was relieved that something was finally being done about it.

"We're going to begin so," said the God-like voice in the room.

A CT scan, which determines the size, shape and location of the tumour, is transferred to the CyberKnife system. Then a machine starts clicking and humming, and the CyberKnife's computer-controlled robotic arm starts moving slowly around you.

Then you hear a 'zzz zzz' noise like a giant, angry wasp as it zaps the tumour with ten times the dose of conventional radiation. It moves around to get it from every angle with the accuracy of a millionth of a centimetre. You feel nothing throughout the treatment.

Each treatment session will last anywhere between 45 and 90 minutes, depending on the tumour. The real difficulty is staying still. With all those X-ray cameras on you, they can tell if you even scratch your nose.

"Are you OK, John?" the disembodied voice will ask if you move an inch.

It's private hospital speak for "Don't you dare move again!"

They scheduled five consecutive days of treatment that week. I had treatment from Monday to Wednesday but on the fourth day, the CyberKnife machine wouldn't work.

I was still in dreadful pain. I was taking the occasional swig of Oramorph to make the pain bearable, but I try to use it as little as possible. The morphine is effective, but it's also addictive, and the longer you take it, the less efficient it becomes at relieving pain.

I went back to the hotel while the hospital waited for an engineer and a machine part to be flown in from Germany to fix the fault. The machine still wasn't fixed the following day, Friday, so I went back to Galway.

I came back to Dublin on Monday again, hoping against hope that the system was working again. They need to administer the course of treatment within a certain amount of days.

The hospital said I might have to fly abroad to complete the treatment if they didn't have it working again by then. It's the kind of stress and uncertainty that no one needs especially when in severe pain. Thankfully, they fixed the machine, and I had the final two days of treatment finishing on September 16th, my 38th birthday.

"Have you any idea when I should start to feel the effects of the treatment?" I asked. "I don't want to stay on steroids or have to keep taking Oramorph. The last thing I need is to get addicted to this stuff."

"We don't know for sure if it will work on this tumour at all," explained Dr Jamsari Khalid or 'Jam' as he tells patients to call him. "But so far we've had good results so I'd be optimistic it will work. Just give it a bit of time."

There was little relief in pain in the following days. I was beginning to worry that it had no effect on the tumour.

After a week, however, the pain levels began to reduce. I found I could walk with less pain and the pronounced limp that I had, started to disappear. All the symptoms began to fade and within weeks, I felt better again. The treatment was working.

I had to wait three months to have the next MRI to check the CyberKnife's effectiveness. Around Christmas, I went to the Galway Clinic for the scan. A friend of mine, Dr Anna Marie O'Connell, is a radiologist in University Hospital Galway.

Anna Marie often reads my scans in advance of my appointments with the consultants. It's great to have friends like Anna Marie. There's nothing worse than knowing the scan results are in, but you can't get them until you can see your consultant after the bank holiday weekend.

I'd rather know, even if it were bad news than live on a knife-edge wondering for days. The results always seem to arrive on Fridays and this occasion was no different. This time, however, Anna Marie said she was unable to help.

"Sorry, John, I haven't had time to check the scan. I'll have to let you know on Monday."

It set alarm bells ringing in my head. Anna Marie will always go to a lot of trouble to read these scans for me. I suspected she had seen the results but wasn't telling me.

"Sh*t," I thought. "This can't be good."

I still hadn't received an appointment from the hospital to get the results by Monday so I rang Anna Marie again.

"Yes, I read it last week," she admitted. "But I didn't want to leave you with this kind of news late on a Friday."

"I knew you read the scan so I've been thinking the worst anyway," I said. "Tell me what it is."

"The tumour which received the CyberKnife has grown, but only by a small amount," she explained. "It may just be swelling from the treatment, but the real problem is that the MRI has shown up another tumour on your spine. This one could cause you serious problems because of where it's positioned."

I thought back to my conversation with consultant radiologist Frank Sullivan a few months earlier. He had mentioned 'new spots further up the spine'. It was only then that I copped on that 'spots' meant more tumours.

Anna Marie added: "Frank will need to go through your options."

The next day, Frank reviewed the MRI and confirmed the news. He also dashed my hopes of avoiding surgery.

"It's really the best option to tackle this tumour," he insisted.

In the New Year, I went back to Dublin's Beaumont Hospital to talk to Dr David O'Brien.

"Of course, the plan is to try to remove as much of this tumour as possible," he said. "Then we recommend a course of radiation to the parts of the spine which haven't been done before. This should prevent any more recurrences."

All I could think of was: "Here we go again. Happy New Year, John."

I didn't feel any ill effects from this new tumour, so I was very reluctant to face more surgery. Yet, I couldn't ignore the advice of the medical profession. I was back on David's operating table in May 2015.

Afterwards, he revealed the tumour had grown considerably since the last scan in December.

"We didn't expect it to be as big as it was," he said. "We didn't get it all out, but we got as much of it as we could, and hopefully the radiation will do the job on the rest."

As a result of the surgery, I had an opportunity to take part in a new gene sequencing research project in Beaumont. Experts believe cancer treatment based on DNA tests could become the norm within five years. So far, trials have shown that using DNA tests, they can shrink tumours at six times the rates of conventional medicine.

Thanks to Frank Sullivan's research connections, they agreed to send a researcher to the theatre to collect a fresh sample of my tumour as it was removed.

Doctors who see patients with rare tumours are often unsure of which treatments will work.

The idea with gene sequencing is that once they identify the DNA of the tumour, the guesswork is eliminated. The doctors will simply prescribe drugs based on the genes in the cancer patients' tumours. It's all about finding the right key to unlock the secrets of each tumour.

They brought the tissue taken from my tumour to the lab and extracted the DNA to sequence it.

It was tested to see if it reacted to any of an extensive catalogue of drugs. Unfortunately, my tumour resisted all of the drugs tested.

Nevertheless, the treatment is expected to be a huge step forward in the battle with cancer in the next few years.

The same day they operated on me in Beaumont, my dad's younger brother, Luke Walsh, died after a long battle with a rare blood cancer in London.

I was determined to get out of the hospital at the end of the week and to go to his funeral in Galway. All my family would be gathering to pay their final respects, and I wanted to be there too.

I began parading the corridor any time David O'Brien was on his rounds that week.

"I'm feeling grand, David. I just need to be signed out so I can go to my uncle's funeral," I said.

I lied. I was doing well, but I wasn't feeling grand. Still, there was no point in being stuck in the hospital any longer. Life is too short, and I'd been doing this too long, and I wanted to go home.

They couldn't start radiation for six to eight weeks after surgery to allow the wound to heal so I would be free of hospitals until then.

I decided I had my fill of hospital wards, doctors' appointments and waiting rooms. From now on, I wanted to be able to spend as much time as possible with family and friends.

In the end, I made it back to Galway in time for Luke's funeral. I didn't stride into the church like anyone else my age; I crept like a 90-year-old.

I'm as proud as any man, but I no longer cared how I looked. I just wanted to be part of normal life, even if normal life means a family funeral. They kept a seat for me near the front of the church, and they padded it with cushions to protect my back.

All through the service, I imagine friends and family wondering to themselves, Luke's gone, who's next?

Looking at me, I doubt anyone guessed it would be my father.

SAORLA & DAD

The birth of our daughter, Saorla, is inextricably linked with my father's death. As our little miracle came into this world, her grandfather stepped into the next world. Happily for us, he returned for a short while to see his granddaughter before he left us forever.

Saorla really is our miracle baby. When Fírinne was born in 2011, I started a chemotherapy drug called Cisplatin. Doctors told us that the chances of conceiving naturally after the treatment were zero.

We felt prepared because Fírinne was already born and we had embryos in storage at the clinic. We had a much-loved child, and we had the chance of more. Ríain was to come two years later from one of those precious embryos.

Then four years after the chemo treatment, when we never dreamed it could happen, Saorla was naturally conceived. I keep winning these million to one lotteries, but this was the best lotto surprise of all.

Her birth may have been the easiest of our three children, but it coincided with a traumatic time for the family.

Edel went through the pregnancy with her customary ease, but there were some slight concerns over Saorla during the pregnancy because she was smaller than she should have been.

On December 22nd, 2015, one week past her due date, Edel had another check-up. The scan revealed the baby had stopped growing so the doctors decided it was time to induce.

Edel had only come to the hospital for a clinic appointment and hadn't brought her labour bag. Our home in Salthill is only a ten-minute walk from the hospital so the midwife told us we could slip out if we were quick.

Edel went upstairs to pack her things. She was upset by the news that the baby had stopped putting on weight three weeks earlier. I rang my mother to tell her we were going to the hospital to have the baby.

I didn't get a chance to say a word.

"John! Who told you?" she said.

"Told me what?"

"My God, it's the agony in the garden here," she replied.

They were her exact words.

"Mam, what are you on about?"

"It's your dad. We're in Galway Clinic. He's stopped breathing, but the doctors are trying to resuscitate him."

Edel came rushing down with her bag at that moment.

"John, for God's sake, do you always have to be on the phone?"

Then she saw my face and realised there was a second emergency in the family.

My mind was racing, and I felt torn in two. I needed to see my father in one hospital, but I needed to be with an upset Edel in another hospital.

Edel made up my mind for me. She told me to drop her at University Hospital Galway and head off to see Dad.

"I'm sure it'll take a while for the labour to get going, just try and be back as soon as you can," she said.

I dropped Edel outside at the maternity unit and sped 15 minutes to the Galway Clinic in Doughiska where Dad was.

My mother explained that she found Dad in severe stomach pain that morning. She rang their GP and once he heard the symptoms, said he needed to get to the hospital immediately.

Both my mother, with her background as a nurse, and the doctor thought it might be a gallstone.

"Don't wait for an ambulance, bring him in now," he instructed.

My uncle Gabriel, and my mother got him into a car and drove to the nearest hospital, which was the Galway Clinic. The pain appeared to subside a bit, and for a while, he was even able to chat.

It was just a brief reprieve, however, because his condition deteriorated rapidly and he collapsed inside the door of the hospital. The staff rushed him to the resuscitation area of the hospital.

By the time I got there, one of my sisters had joined my mother in the waiting room. A doctor arrived after half an hour to give Mam an update on Dad's condition. The news was grim.

"He has a ruptured aneurism in his abdomen, and it sent him into cardiac arrest," he explained.

We mentally prepared ourselves for the worst. I rang Edel to see how she was and to update her on the situation.

My sister was despondent as she spoke to me out of earshot of our mother.

"Dad's not going to need us here for long by the sounds of things," she said. "You'll be able to get back to Edel soon."

My heart thumped when the doctor re-emerged 15 minutes later, and I steeled myself for the worst.

"We resuscitated Patrick, but we can't stabilise his condition here," he said. "We need to get him to University Hospital for emergency surgery."

He revealed the prognosis was not good. They weren't sure he could even survive the ambulance journey.

"Transferring him to another hospital in his condition is risky. It's 50-50 that he'll make it to another hospital, but we have no choice. Surgery is his only chance of survival."

One of us asked his chances of coming out of the surgery alive. There was no good news.

"He's gravely ill," he said. "There's a good chance that he might not make it. Even if he does survive the surgery, there's still a high chance he could die from complications of the operation."

I drove back to University Hospital to Edel as they made arrangements to transfer Dad.

Edel was advised to walk around during labour, so we were pacing the corridors when we overheard a surgeon on his phone:

"Emergency transfer from the Galway Clinic? What time? 4.30pm, OK," he said as he passed.

We knew my dad was on his way. I ran down to the ambulance bay to meet him. I was able to call my mother and let her know that he'd survived the journey and was in surgery.

That evening my head was in two places. I was with Edel in the delivery room watching new life being born.

Meanwhile, I was running to my family upstairs in the waiting room to hear news of my dad who was possibly dying. I didn't know where I should be that night.

As it happened, my father came out of surgery just before Saorla was born.

Our perfect Christmas present flew into the world eager to meet everyone around 9.00pm. She was the smallest of our babies weighing in at 6lb 3oz, but she had a good set of lungs and yelled gustily at everyone.

I spent a half an hour with Edel and Saorla and then ran upstairs to see if there was any update on dad before running down to the girls again.

Dad was still on life support and in intensive care when Edel and Saorla left the hospital two days later. His doctors admitted there was a possibility of brain damage after the lengthy resuscitation. Nobody seemed confident of his chances.

Despite the odds, as the days went on, we got more hopeful. Dad proved he was a fighter.

Living and working close to the hospital meant I was able to visit Dad before work, during lunchtime and after work. I'd go home for a while and go back to the hospital again to see him at night.

It was hard for Edel though. We had a new baby and between work and visiting dad, I was scarcely at home to help out.

On St Stephen's Day, four days after his admission, I dropped in to see Dad at 11.00pm but found him surrounded by a flurry of medical staff.

A doctor took me aside.

"Your father's stats have gone right down which could indicate infection," he said. "We need you to sign a consent form because we need to do surgery immediately."

"Surgery? Do you think he's able for another operation?"

"I'm afraid we don't have any choice," he said.

They took him away, and the family arrived expecting the worst to happen. The surgeon came to see us afterwards.

"We operated, but we couldn't find any reason for the abnormal readings. It's not what we thought it was."

His stats stabilised once he was back in intensive care but there were dramas like this for weeks.

There were conflicting opinions about his condition all the time. I'd meet the cardiac consultant and he'd tell me: "Your father is doing great, John!"

Then I'd meet another professional in a white coat who'd shake his head and say: "It's not looking good at this stage, John."

We didn't know what to believe. Then he started to make huge strides when they gave him a tracheostomy to help his breathing. He started showing signs of coming around.

About three weeks after he was admitted, I arrived at Dad's bedside for my usual lunchtime visit. He was still non-responsive, but I always bought a newspaper to read to him.

That day, the papers were sold out in the hospital shop, and I could only pick up an English tabloid. I started flicking through the pages to read to him, but I could see no news that would appeal to him.

"A gangland murder in Dublin on the front page," I said. "That won't interest you. Oh look, on page three, someone we've never heard of has got a new boob job. I don't think I'll find the price of a ewe hogget in here, Dad."

After flicking through another few pages, I groaned in exasperation.

"There's nothing at all to read in this paper. What did I buy this sh**e for?" I said.

Out of nowhere, he raised his hand from the bed and shoved the newspaper. He was trying to ask me the same thing! It was the first indication that I had that he was on the road to recovery.

Soon after I was able to show him my phone and say, "Hey Dad, you've got a new granddaughter." He clutched my hands as I held the phone, and he turned it this way and that and squinted at the screen to have a good look at Saorla.

The hospital was able to put a speaking valve into the tracheostomy to allow him to talk, and he was happier after that.

"Ah, I'd say I'm middling," he'd say when we asked him how he felt.

We had great hope at that stage that he had turned a corner and was recovering. His doctors spoke about reducing the medication and moving him to the high dependency ward.

I was with him on the night of Tuesday, January 19th and he was in good form when I left.

I accidentally left my phone in the kitchen instead of bringing it to bed with me. I must have been mentally relaxing because I hadn't dared to leave it out of my sight before that. For weeks, I had been expecting to get that call that would tell me to get to the hospital for the last time. Now, I felt, he was definitely on the mend.

The next morning, I went downstairs, picked up my phone and saw nine missed calls from the Intensive Care Unit and seven missed calls from my mother.

I knew straight away.

I went and had a shower. It was my own way of keeping the bad news at arm's length. But then Edel came rushing in with her phone. My mother called her when she couldn't get me.

"John, you need to take this - it's your mother!"

I didn't want to take the phone because that would make it true.

"Hi Mam."

"John, it's your dad, he's gone."

"I know," I said.

He survived a month but on the morning of Wednesday, January 20th, 2016, at 7.36am, he passed away while he slept.

The only consolation I had was that he hadn't died on December 22nd when he first collapsed.

Only about 1 in 5 people survive a ruptured abdominal aneurysm so we were lucky to have a month with him at all. We were especially fortunate to have a week where he was conscious and where we were all there to let him know he was loved and let him know how much he meant to us.

I arrived at Dad's hospital bed within a half hour while Mam was still on her way. I had a final hour with Dad, holding his hands and talking to him and recalling some of my fondest memories.

I remember my father as a reserved and intelligent man but also, a real character, who had a genuine interest in everyone. If you met him, he'd quiz you until he found out what you were doing, who you were related to and who you both knew in common.

His comfort zone was Liskeavy, Milltown and Galway and he'd no desire to spend any time beyond their boundaries. He was happy at home.

He always put family first and was an uncomplaining taxi man for his kids and a piggyback ride for his grandchildren.

As a child, I loved going out in the car with him and I'd beg him to drive really fast. I used to call him Knight Rider after the popular TV series of the time and of course, I was his sidekick, KITT.

I thought my dad was the greatest.

I recalled how he never gave out to us for anything. I could wreck his car or his lawn mower (and I did both), and he'd say nothing. He just had this doleful way of looking at you that made you feel disappointed in yourself.

He was a devoted Fianna Failer and Charlie Haughey's visit to Milltown in the 80's was one of the best days of his life. He was loyal to the last even about much-maligned party leaders like Charlie and Bertie Ahern.

"Sure they were great men," he'd say.

That was Dad; he'd stand up for all of us in times of trouble and defend his friends and family to the last.

There were no tears during my last hour alone with Dad. I recalled my fondest memories of us together, and he looked so peaceful that he could have been listening with his eyes closed.

It wasn't a surprise to me that he died a relatively young man. He was a chain smoker with a 50-a-day habit, and he never saw a doctor.

Neither the GP nor the hospital had a file on him. Maybe he thought he was invincible, but it was more likely that he didn't want to be told to stop smoking. He may also have been afraid of what he might learn if he had a check-up.

I gave the eulogy for Dad at his funeral in St Joseph's Church in Milltown three days later.

I reminded his friends and family that being an electrician, he had spent his whole working life turning on the light for other people. It was his turn that day, I said, for God's light to shine brightly on him.

The tools he used to create the miracle of light - his phase tester, red snips, pliers and a torch - featured in the offertory procession. He was laid to rest in Kilgevrin Cemetery in Milltown on a cold January day.

Just last weekend I was at my parents' house, and I noticed that the grass was growing high. Dad always looked after the garden and just a few months after his death, it's starting to look unkempt.

I decided to take out the mower on Sunday to tackle the lawn. In the past, whenever I cut the lawn, he'd sit out on the garden bench and supervise proceedings. I'd see him craning his neck to watch my every move.

Even though I wouldn't be able to hear him over the mower, he'd gesture and point to direct me towards bits that weren't done properly.

Last Sunday, while I mowed, I looked over at the garden bench, and I could still see him.

He was sitting there, laughing and waving at me, and pointing where I missed a spot.

BACK PROBLEMS

We always knew the surgery wouldn't remove the entire second tumour on my spine. Dr David O'Brien just took out as much as he could in May 2015 and it was always part of my care plan to have radiation three months later.

The idea was to radiate any parts of the spine not already irradiated to curtail any further spread. Physically, it took me a month to get over the surgery, and I got back to work in June.

Everything appeared fine. It was a bit of a pain that radiation was still hanging over me for the summer but I just thought, 'let's do it and just get it over with'.

I had a post-operative scan in July and Edel, and I went to David O'Brien's office in Beaumont Hospital in Dublin for the results. He had to check that the surgical wound was healed and give the go ahead for radiation in Galway.

David was full of lavish praise for how well I was getting on and how amazingly well I seemed after the operation. I lapped up the applause as my due and basked in the glory. Yes, I was feeling fantastic; feeling terrific in fact. I was a medical marvel. Sure, why wouldn't I be feeling great?

Edel wasn't fooled and admitted afterwards that her heart was sinking as he spoke. She always gets nervous when doctors start off with fulsome praise or if they're full of positivity. She feels it's a precursor to bad news, and that good cheer is always followed by the big 'but' or the 'however'.

So while I was grinning ear-to-ear, she was thinking: "Oh, God, are the results that bad?"

David began by going through the results of the scan. He started referring to tumours on the T2, T3, T4 and L1 and other mysterious parts of the spine.

I was under the impression I now had two tumours in my back. Edel and I looked at each other because it certainly sounded like there were a lot more.

I didn't want to know, but I asked anyway: "Just how many tumours are there?"

David looked at me and then looked down and started reading the file on his desk.

"One, two, three…five…six…" he said running his finger down the page. Then he turned the page and appeared to count more.

"Oh, there's a few more there, and there's a thickening of lining there that can be disease, or it could be surgical scarring, but there may be other spots…"

Edel and I looked at each other in utter shock and David never finished the count. We were panicked leaving Dublin that day and couldn't talk for about an hour afterwards.

I had expected the radiation to clean up anything left over from the tumour surgery in May. I had thought of it as a precautionary measure to stop the tumour in its tracks. I hadn't expected to be faced with many multiples of additional growths.

That month I began six weeks of daily radiation under Frank Sullivan in University Hospital Galway in July. Once I was over the shock results of the scan, I felt optimistic. I was well and had no symptoms at all.

It's always a balancing act between work and getting to my hospital appointments, but I managed to work through most of it. It's good to lead as normal a life as you can during treatment. For me, it's not healthy being home and staring at the four walls. I prefer being at work and just taking off the occasional day when I feel completely wiped by the treatment.

After the news that the tumours were spreading on the spine, I began to think it might be a good time to seek another second opinion. It had been three years since I'd been to Memorial Sloan Kettering Cancer Centre in New York and I thought it would be timely to see if there were any new treatment options abroad that might help.

Then a friend in Boston revealed that a doctor from Sloan Kettering, who is also a friend of his, was coincidentally on his way to Ireland.

Fellow Irishman, Dr Patrick Boland, was due to fly from New York to perform an operation in Galway. My friend thought it might be the perfect opportunity for another opinion and to see if I was still getting the best treatment for my type of cancer.

Dr Boland is a specialist in bone cancer, but he agreed to meet with me, take my files and scans back to Sloan Kettering and discuss my case with all the relevant consultants in New York.

With my bulky medical records under my arm, I went to meet him in the hospital foyer in Galway at the appointed time and day.

He looked surprised when I introduced myself, and I wondered if he was expecting to meet someone else. He told me afterwards that he'd looked at my charts, and was looking for someone in a wheelchair

Most people seem to be surprised at how active I look after they read my medical file. Edel organised all the scans and pages for him and said she was upset for two days afterwards, and she wasn't even trying to read them. They don't make good reading.

We went through the treatments that I'd had, and he compared CyberKnife to a spot weld. It fixes a single problem, but he said you need something more systemic like chemo to mop up everything that can pop up everywhere else. It was the first time I'd heard of CyberKnife compared to spot welding.

He brought my files back to America and met with all the consultants in Sloan Kettering. Then he phoned me two or three weeks later, and said they had looked at the files, but there were no new trials or treatments available. Once again, it was confirmed that I was getting the best treatment available. That, in itself, was reassuring.

After the six weeks of radiation finished at the end of August, I had a follow-up scan in October. That scan showed that spread of tumours had halted. Nothing had changed, but there were no new or active tumours, and none of the existing tumours had grown. It seemed as if the radiation had put everything on ice.

Edel was in the last stages of her pregnancy with our third baby, and we thought we'd be able to breathe again for a while. Instead, we had a chaotic few weeks as the birth of Saorla coincided with the sudden critical illness and death of my father.

We were still reeling from those traumatic weeks when a routine scan in Galway University Hospital in February 2016 brought more bad news.

The radiation hadn't worked as everyone hoped and the tumours were on the move again. I wasn't prepared for the news because I hadn't felt any ill effects.

The scan showed the tumour that they had operated on and radiated last year was growing again. There were also new 'spots' further up the spine.

Worse still, two new spots had shown up in my brain, the first recurrence since in my head since radiation in 2005. That came as a complete shock to me. After eleven years, I didn't expect to be hearing that news again.

It was grim news all round and our usual go-to-guy, Frank, had just left his position at Galway University

Hospital to dedicate more time to research and teaching.

At this stage, I was starting to hear softly spoken observations from the consultants that my options, regarding treatments, were starting to dwindle. They never said I was out of options, but they certainly suggested that I was running out of them.

It was a blow to learn that radiating the entire spine in the summer of 2015 hadn't worked. The problem is there are lifetime limits of radiation, and once an area is irradiated, they can't do it again.

The spinal cord, in particular, can't take as much radiation as other parts of the body such as the brain. The dosage is quite limited from the outset. It felt like we'd now played our radiation card and lost it.

Surgery is also a hazardous option as the spine has already been operated on three times and weakened further by CyberKnife treatment and traditional radiation.

Dr Clare Faul, who's a radiation oncologist in Beaumont, the Mater Private and the Hermitage hospitals in Dublin, is now involved in my treatment.

A sparky, bright-eyed Irish woman in her fifties with auburn bobbed hair, I first met with Clare in 2005. She first recommended that I should receive radiotherapy after my second brain surgery. Thankfully she referred me to the new radiation centre that had just opened in Galway that year, so I didn't have to travel to Dublin for that, and I hadn't seen her since.

I made it clear that I didn't want to go for another operation on the spine, and I certainly didn't want to go for another surgery on my brain. I was relieved when she said that a second round of CyberKnife radiation in the Hermitage Medical Clinic was an option.

She wanted to concentrate on the two small tumours on my brain - one was 10mm, and one was 7mm, so they were relatively small.

She also wanted to focus on getting rid of a couple of spots that were growing on my spine near my neck that could cause problems in the future.

My second bout of CyberKnife treatment began in April. Unlike the last time I had CyberKnife, I had no obvious symptoms so it was a walk in the park. Compared to surgery or chemo or even traditional radiation, CyberKnife is a dream.

You just let the laser and the X-ray cameras do their work. Because it's so targeted, you don't have any concerns that it's damaging the healthy tissue around the tumour either. It's quick and easy, and it doesn't require a hospital stay. Of course, the only place it's available is in the Hermitage so it meant staying in a Dublin hotel for the ten days of treatment.

I had seven days of CyberKnife to the back and three days of it to the brain. Clare said it would take a few months before I'd discover if the treatment worked.

She also suggested that we start looking into a palliative form of oral chemotherapy drug. It involves taking chemo pills daily with the aim of stopping any further tumour growth or at least, slowing the progress.

I was a bit surprised to hear that chemo was back on the cards because they said in 2014 that my sort of tumour didn't respond to chemo.

However, chemo is back as an option because the tumours are behaving differently now and growing faster than they did in the past.

Clare referred me to Dr Patrick Morris, the oncologist in Beaumont, who had remembered my case from his days in Sloan Kettering Memorial in New York.

"There are two types we can use depending on how well the tumours respond to the CyberKnife treatment," he explained. "One is a light form of chemo called Temozolomide. It's a mild dose, and there's no hair loss and minimum tiredness. Then there's a second one that is stronger, a combination of Carboplatin and Etoposide. That one will have side effects including, possibly, hair loss and sickness."

Happily, my latest the scan result at the end of July was positive. I was able to breathe a little easier when Edel and I heard that the tumours are still there but there was no new active growth.

The CyberKnife hadn't eliminated the ones on the brain as Clare had earlier hoped but it did succeed in zapping a few on the spine that she was concerned about and has halted the growth for now.

Now I'm awaiting a decision on the form of chemo I'll be getting. I don't want to lose my hair. Apart from any vanity involved, I think losing my hair would be hard for the kids. That's something that I couldn't hide from them, and I don't want to expose them to unnecessary worry for as long as I can.

JOHN WALSH

FALLOUT

There's a sign on the wall in The Galway Clinic that I've photographed and kept on my phone. It reads: 'Health is a crown worn by those who are well and seen only by the sick.' It's an old Syrian proverb, and it's one that resonates with me.

When I see people talking and laughing, I often envy their carefree existence and the life that people have when they can take good health for granted. I feel like an outsider, looking in; that I'm getting a glimpse of what it is to have a normal life.

I join in all the jollity but sometimes it's a front; a happy mask. The only time the mask comes off is when I talk to others in the same position as me because I feel they're the only ones who understand what it's like living in the shadow of an incurable disease.

I don't think about it all the time, but I do wonder why I was the one picked out for this path or to make this journey. I try not to think about it too much, but it does cross your mind, 'why me?'

When I see younger adults with cancer, in particular, I empathise with them. There's nothing worse for a young person who has just started to gain their independence, to lose it all again to cancer.

Worse still, they have no idea of the many struggles they'll face in the years ahead.

There's no denying that having a life-threatening illness has had an enormous ripple effect on my life and that of my wife and family. We try to live a normal life, but we have a different version of 'normal' in our house.

Illness has had a huge impact financially on a family. There are the obvious medical costs, but we've faced lots of other unforeseen costs too down through the years.

For any young adult, it has the potential to reduce job prospects for years. It's never a good time to get a brain tumour or any chronic illness, but it happened to me at a time when everyone is supposed to be building their lives and careers.

By the time I reached my mid-20s, everyone I knew was getting job promotions or moving jobs and thinking about buying houses. I was still battling depression and looking for an entry-level job.

It was like everyone else my age had moved on while I was trying to kick-start my life. The big black hole of a year on my C.V. prompted questions, and when I had to reveal that I had to leave my job because of a brain tumour, prospective employers seemed to melt away. Nobody wants to hire anyone with potential health problems.

I'm blessed that the first job opportunity I got was with the public service body, The HSE and now I'm working with the state agency, Tusla.

My employers have always been accommodating and understanding about taking time out for treatment.

Anyone in my position in the private sector or self-employed would find it difficult to hold down jobs if they need time off for repeated procedures.

At the same time, I'm very conscious of taking time off. Public sector workers are allowed three months sick leave on full pay over the past four years. That can be extended, on an exceptional basis, to six months sick leave over the previous four years if you have a critical illness. It means treatment that I've had from 2012 onwards has an impact on my eligible sick leave this year. It's just an added worry when you're liable to fall ill at any time.

Edel and I faced another financial hurdle when we went to buy our first real family house in 2011. We discovered our borrowing capacity was restricted because I couldn't get life insurance for a mortgage. It's something you don't think about until you're faced with it.

Again, I'm more fortunate than most others in my position because public service workers have something called Death in Service Benefit. It means that a year's salary is guaranteed if I die while still working for the public service. It gave the banks some guarantee that my share of the mortgage could be paid back upon my premature death.

Still, anyone suffering from long-term illness with a mortgage will wryly smile at all the advice about switching your mortgage for a better deal. We're stuck with the rate we have and can't ever consider a change.

We were lucky to get a mortgage at all, and no one is going to take on someone as risky as me now.

Fertility problems are another obstacle for young people with cancer and may have significant cost implications for the future. IVF set us back financially for a long time in the early years of our marriage, and it's a burden that we'd probably never have encountered if not for my illness and treatment.

Medical care is expensive but thankfully it's not a major issue for us. Thanks to a discretionary medical card and private health insurance, I manage to cover most of my costs. However, the medical card wasn't handed to me and, like many, I had a long and hard fight to get it and to keep it.

Obviously, dropping private medical insurance is not an option either. If I hadn't got that insurance, I wouldn't have been able to access the private Hermitage Clinic and the CyberKnife treatment that's now saving my life. But it's a sobering thought that there are people out there being deprived of that treatment because they can't afford medical insurance.

Other day-to-day medical costs of a long-term illness that aren't covered by insurance include travel expenses to and from hospitals. If you live outside of the major cities also becomes a major expense.

It's not just the unexpected and on-going costs of a long-term illness that affect a family. Like I said, I'm fortunate to be able to work, but we have to keep an eye to a time when I might not be able to work.

When people our age save, it's usually for a family holiday, a new kitchen or a car. When we try to put money away, we save for when I might be too sick to work. Both of us need to work to meet the bills and to look after the needs of three pre-school children. Taking part-time employment or parental leave while the kids are young is another luxury that Edel feels she can't afford.

We also save in case a new treatment emerges that health insurance won't cover or if I need to travel abroad for a trial or treatment that's not available here. There is always that underlying sense of vulnerability because we never know what's around the corner.

Another benefit of being in a public service job is that you automatically pay into their Spouses' & Children's Scheme as soon as you have a child. It's not worth a lot, but when I look at my payslip every two weeks, it makes me feel good to see the balance is growing all the time. I think that's a little more that I can leave to Edel and the kids if anything happens to me. Not everyone else in my position has that bit of reassurance.

The unexpected costs of cancer are not all financial either. No one anticipates the mental and emotional toll that a critical illness exacts on a person. That constant state of fear can wear you down. You and your partner grieve for the future that you have lost together. You dread the next ache or pain that may or may not indicate another tumour.

There are days when the scan results are gloomy, or you're in the throes of pain or treatment, it's a constant mental battle to stay sane.

Any life-threatening experience leaves an emotional and psychological legacy for years. For a long time, my health suffered more from anxiety and depression over the illness rather than any illness itself.

Looking back, I realise I suffered from post-traumatic stress after my diagnosis. But when it happened to me, I didn't recognise it. I had never been told that a significant life crisis, like having a brain tumour could result in these feelings.

The medical profession largely ignores the psychological needs of patients. If I'd been warned about the psychological side-effects to having a life-threatening condition, my younger years would have been far less traumatic.

Even today, while there's a lot more awareness of depression, it's left to the charity organisations, such as Cancer Care West, to provide emotional support and care for patients. It still hasn't become an integral part of medical care that it should be.

Illness doesn't just have a mental and emotional toll on me, as Edel feels the stress of it all too. Not only is she always worrying about me, but also she worries about what will happen if something happened to her.

I don't know how I'd cope if she got sick or injured; financially, we couldn't cope at all. But that's one too many things for me to worry about so I don't even go there.

Families with someone suffering from a chronic illness are different too because we can never plan anything. We can never book a holiday for example. And when people invite us to events in the future, we are always non-committal. If there's a wedding abroad next year, we can't book until the last minute. We just don't know what's going to happen tomorrow never mind next year.

One day last week I couldn't breathe and had chest pain and ended up back in the hospital. At first, they thought I had a blood clot in my lungs, and then they diagnosed it as pain from the radiation that's compressing my bones.

One day I'm perfectly well and the next I'm on a hospital trolley. We can't plan our lives so we just don't.

It's in my nature to be optimistic and have a positive outlook. I like putting a smile on people's faces, and I'm never a miserable person, but it's hard to feel upbeat all the time.

When anyone ill hears words like 'incurable', 'inoperable, 'life-limiting', 'terminal', 'malignant' or even 'cancer, it's hard to have a zest for life.

When there's an interminable wait for test results, when you're queuing in a doctor's surgery, or facing surgery or watching the drip, drip, drip of chemo into your veins for hours on end, it's not easy to find your mojo.

At the same time, there's almost a tyranny of positive thinking imposed on the sick. We're told we should think only happy thoughts and that we'll feel better if we wear a sunny smile. There's always someone well-meaning who'll tell you that there are lots of people worse off than you. It only serves to pile more pressure on anyone who's sick, anxious or depressed. They're made to feel inadequate because they're not all happy-clappy and psyched-up for the challenge of cancer.

No matter how positive you are, there are always going to be dark and dismal days when the fallout gets too much.

And there are days when you just want to feel normal, but you despair knowing that you'll never feel that way again.

These are the days when you just want to pull the covers over your head and stay in bed. And there are days when you should do just that.

One of the things I've learned over the years is that sometimes you have to give yourself permission to say: 'I'll be OK, just not today'.

THE FUTURE

If asked how I'm feeling these days, I tell people I feel like a house on fire. Everyone around me is manning the hoses, but as soon as they manage to extinguish one fire, two fires break out elsewhere. In the past two years especially, it always seems to be an emergency situation.

We don't have any roadmap for the future, and we don't know what is going on day to day now. Constant challenges are being thrown in the way especially since 2014. The interventions are getting more frequent and the time lapse between each intervention is getting shorter. The consultants have made it clear that my options are dwindling.

I know I'm ill, yet I'm feeling well at the moment. At the same time, I'm constantly alert because this could be the calm before the next medical storm hits.

I know there are other more radical options out there if the conventional medical ones don't work. There's always the guinea pig route, where you start joining trials like the ones they do in Sloan Kettering in New York. But do I want to spend six months away from my kids when there's no guarantee of the trial working? I don't think so.

There's a local nun who recommended a faith healer called John of God or João de Deus in Brazil. He claims to be a medium and psychic surgeon who sees thousands of visitors every week from all over the world. Being a spiritual person, rather than a religious one, I think I'd prefer to exhaust all traditional medicine options first.

I've another friend who recommended a 'healing journey' to a clean eating and detox centre in Mexico that advocates non-toxic treatment for cancer and other chronic degenerative diseases. I haven't gone down the route of seeds, sprouts and superfoods yet. I'm not into juicing or drinking green sludge every morning, but lots of other people recommend it, so who knows? I might try it. Although the last I heard about from my clean-eating friend, he was back in the hospital.

Someone else suggested cannabis oil and there was something in the Washington Post that showed taking it with radiation showed promising results. There's an endless array of non-conventional and alternative health routes that you could take if you are desperate enough.

Still, I think one of the best ways of facing the future is to keep things simple, follow your doctors' advice and keep a positive and optimistic mind-set. However, to stay positive, you need a lot of coping strategies.

Most people have the luxury of thinking about death in the abstract; as something that will happen to them in the far distant future. When there's a black tumour cloud always hovering over your shoulder and death becomes a very real possibility, it's harder to stay upbeat.

One of my coping strategies is to avoid Dr Google and to avoid seeking medical information on the internet. It's not that I want to be ignorant about what's going on, but I avoid online information because it tends to highlight the worst-case scenario.

If you read the small print on a box of Aspirin or paracetamol, you'd probably be afraid to take a headache pill again. There is such a thing as too much information, so I try to avoid it.

I'm not medically trained to decipher any of it accurately so I feel such information raises more questions than it answers. The tumours I have are so rare that there's little reliable information out there anyway.

Anyone who has a life-limiting physical illness knows it can be a very isolating experience. It's like spinning around in an impenetrable dark forest, and not knowing what's going to attack you from where.

I've tried anti-depressants, but I haven't bothered with them in many years because personally, I don't find them effective.

I'm not advocating that anyone else throw their Prozac prescriptions in the bin, but anti-anxiety medication never worked for me for some reason.

One of the most effective coping strategies for me has been support groups and group therapy sessions. When you feel as if no one else understands, it's therapeutic to be around others who are in a similar situation.

In the last few years, Cancer Care West set up a support group with a trained mediator that I found very helpful. Meeting twice a month, it gave many of us the opportunity to share common experiences and to lift the burden of illness.

I haven't been to one in a while because I was swamped with hospital appointments and treatments over the last year. I just let the meetings fall by the wayside, but a support group is something I'll happily join again.

There's a camaraderie that develops very quickly in this kind of unique clique. You discover that everyone else feels the same gnawing anxiety, and many are in the depths of a black depression.

There's shorthand between everyone and we all nod in understanding when someone discusses those long nights when the cold terror of dying keeps you awake.

Tackling anxiety and always living on a knife-edge are issues that are very much to the fore in cancer support groups.

The only hazard of making friends with those who have chronic illnesses is that they sometimes leave your life too soon. Just a few weeks ago, I heard that one of the women in my talk group passed away recently. It was a total shock, as she seemed so healthy the last time I saw her.

I knew the story of her illness, about her issues with work, the things she was worried about, and now she is gone. It adds to the fear. You can't avoid thinking, which one of us is next? But that's something that you can't dwell on for long if you want any quality of life.

Cancer Care West counsellor, Helen Greally, has taught me other helpful stress management techniques. One of those practical aides is cognitive behavioural therapy, which aims to stop you getting into negative thought patterns and improve the way you feel.

She teaches how to recognise when you're getting into a negative cycle and how to stop and ask out loud, 'why am I having these feelings or thoughts?' The problem is you get days where you have negative feelings twenty times a day, and addressing all those issues can be exhausting.

She also promotes a technique called the body scan, a mindfulness meditation practice that helps you to become more aware of your body and becoming more 'present'.

It doesn't work for me because I haven't got the concentration levels to focus on the facilitator's instructions. When I'm being told to control my breathing and to visualise a lovely flower by a stream, I'm wondering 'what time is that match at?'

It seems to work for many other people as a relaxation technique, but when I lie down on a yoga mat, I have 50,000 things racing through my head. I find watching football more relaxing than yoga.

Even though there's a lot of fallout from having a life-limiting disease, it isn't all negative. Many of the wonderful people in my life, for example, would not be here if I hadn't been diagnosed with a brain tumour when I was 23.

If all this didn't happen, I'd probably still be living in Germany. I'd never have seen Edel again nor have enjoyed the life that I've had with her and our three children in Galway. I'd also have never had the circle of friends that I do today if it wasn't for that tumour.

I've met so many inspiring people in hospital wards or waiting rooms or in chemo treatment, with whom I've forged an instant and life-long bond. Cancer and severe illness have a way of linking you to others, and I meet new and inspiring people all the time.

Just last week I met an 80-year-old woman in a hospital corridor who had all the joie de vivre of a teenager. This woman loves life and her two cats with equal passion. We were chatting away, whiling away the time, and sitting amongst the dozen or so elderly heart patients who were also waiting.

Suddenly, the corridor resounded with the clanging guitar riff to Guns N'Roses, Sweet Child O'Mine. Everyone was startled by the noise of Slash's hard rock intro echoing through the hall.

Then the old lady leapt up and raced off down the corridor. Guns N'Roses was the ringtone to the phone she'd left charging down the hall. I don't think I've laughed as much in a long time.

Recently, I met another guy who reminded me how such traumatic events can change your life. Ten years ago, this guy told me he was in a bad way. He was divorced, drinking a lot and he seriously thought about killing himself. Now he insists he's turned his life around. He's a zen person, centred and with a new lease of life.

He took out a pen to take down my phone number but found that his biro wouldn't work.

"See, this is how my life has changed," he explained. "If that was ten years ago I would have got that biro and f***ed it at the wall and screamed 'f*** you biro!'"

Instead, he went over to the waste bin and addressing the pen, he said: "Thank you biro for all your hard work but now you and I must part ways." Then he placed the biro carefully in the bin. He turned around with a beaming smile and said: "See?"

Illness also changed me for the better on a very fundamental level. When I was young, I was a cocky and arrogant guy. It took that diagnosis of a brain tumour to level me and bring me back down to earth.

The cumulative effect of so many medical blows has possibly resulted in lowering my self-esteem even further. There's a certain amount of guilt and self-blame that goes with recurring illness.

But it's fair to say, I'm an entirely different man, and probably a much nicer one, than the man I was then. I have far more empathy with people and far more patience with people in general. I never rush to judge anyone now because there are so many things we don't know about other peoples' lives.

I'm rarely critical or negative about people. I'm not terribly religious, but I have a copy of Pope Francis's

'10 Top Tips for Happiness' and I particularly like number eight which reads: "Needing to talk badly about others indicates low self-esteem. That means, 'I feel so low that instead of picking myself up I have to cut others down.' Letting go of negative things quickly is healthy."

Having a life-limiting or life-threatening disease gives a person a whole new perspective on life. It's a wake-up call that makes me appreciate the important things in life.

I'm not as emotional or as sentimental as I used to be when I was younger, but I'm a much stronger person. Years spent living with illness has made me stronger than I ever thought I could be.

Chronic illness also is a way to make you focus on the here and now. It's the ultimate lesson in mindfulness and living in the present. The future is something Edel and I can't control so we just get on with enjoying each day that we can.

My medical file has grown huge over the past 16 years and makes for scary reading. I've had many major surgeries along with multiple cycles of radiation, chemotherapy and Cyber Knife. I've had 150 radiotherapy appointments in Galway and another 30 in Dublin alone. I'm battle scarred and battle hardened, but I'm still here, and still loving life. They say I'm running out of options now, but I'm still not out of options.

Even though the outlook has been very grim many times in the past, I've not only survived, but I'm still

JOHN WALSH

enjoying a good quality of life. Two years ago, I could barely move and was days away from being in a wheelchair when Cyber Knife surgery saved me. Something that wasn't an option even five years ago is now keeping me alive so you never know what other revolutionary treatment is just around the corner.

Living with illness is not easy, in fact, it's been a huge struggle and seems overwhelming at times, but mostly we manage to live a normal life. Every day is a good day when I can get out of the bed and get the kids ready and go to work.

As far as Edel's concerned, there's nothing that worries her unless it involves my health or the kids'. No other problems faze her.

Meanwhile, I get real joy out of seeing my children grow up and out of people saying what a lovely family I have. I'm thankful that Edel is doing well and coping with the demands of a hectic job, three children and me. The fact that we're still together gives me a high too. Every marriage can be stressful but we've faced some serious hurdles in our lives, not just cancer but IVF, and we've come out the other side.

I'm inspired by that time when Galway won the All-Ireland final in 1998 for the first time in 32 years and manager, John O'Mahony, was asked 'How did you do that?"

He replied: "The team did the simple things well; if you do the simple things right other things follow."

It's such a good mantra to have. Do the simple things well. You can't always choose your circumstances, but you can choose your reaction to the things that happen to you. I choose to keep things simple and go on as long as I can and avail of every treatment there is to survive.

Striving to live a normal life is the most effective coping strategy of all. I'm fortunate that I have a great family life and I'm doing work that I enjoy in Tusla. When you have to get to work every day and get the children to crèche or school, you don't have time to think about yourself or your problems. Living normal life is probably the most simple, cheap and effective survival strategy of all.

I also like to challenge myself and set goals for my day-to-day life. I always have at least a few short and medium term goals in my head. Now that I've seen Fírinne's first day at school, my next goal is to see her First Communion. I've all the kids' milestones in my head and I tick them off as I go along.

Another goal of mine was to write this book. Initially, I thought writing my story would be a lovely way for the children to get an insight into their dad and his life if anything happened to me before they grow up.

It also became both a therapeutic and cathartic process allowing me to reflect on my life, get a perspective on what happened and discover how I've changed and what I've learned along the way.

At the same time, I hope that by doing this I can provide help and inspiration to other people who are facing many of the same challenges that I have.

Maybe by telling my story, other people starting out on this cancer journey, may not be so afraid of the rollercoaster ride ahead.

Because it is a rollercoaster, and it's hair-raising at times, but it's also survivable. It's important to remember that. It's an incredible journey and a very difficult one at times. But most people will survive cancer and maybe, as in my case, might become a better person because of their experiences.

I'm optimistic, but I have to be realistic too. My life has turned into more of a battleground in recent years. This illness has the potential to reduce my life expectancy significantly, and my greatest fear is prematurely leaving my children and my wife.

At the same time, I've managed to survive many times before when the odds seemed stacked against me. I'm encouraged that new cancer treatments and medical advancements are happening all the time.

I know I'm not going to feel strong every day. But right now I can say that I'm filled with hope because life is good and because I have so much to live for.

God's Ways

Pope Francis's 10 Tips for Happiness

1. "Live and let live." Everyone should be guided by this principle and the saying "move forward and let others do the same."
2. "Be giving of yourself to others," he said. People need to be open and generous toward others because "if you withdraw into yourself, you run the risk of becoming egocentric. And stagnant water becomes putrid."
3. "Proceed calmly" in life.
4. Enjoy a healthy sense of leisure. "Consumerism has brought us anxiety," he said. Parents should to set aside time to play with their children and turn off the TV when they sit down to eat.
5. Workers should have Sundays off because "Sunday is for family," he said.
6. Find innovative ways to create dignified jobs for young people. If they have no opportunities they'll get into drugs and be more vulnerable to suicide.
7. Respect and take care of nature. Environmental degradation "is one of the biggest challenges we have."
8. Stop being negative. "Needing to talk badly about others indicates low self-esteem,'' he said. "That means, 'I feel so low that instead of picking myself up I have to cut others down. Letting go of negative things quickly is healthy."
9. Don't proselytise; respect others' beliefs. "We can inspire others through witness. The church grows by attraction, not proselytising," he said.
10. Work for peace. "We are living in a time of many wars," he said. "The call for peace must be shouted. Peace sometimes gives the impression of being quiet, but it is never quiet, peace is always proactive and dynamic."

AUTHOR BIOGRAPHY

John Walsh is 39-years-old and lives in Salthill in Galway. He is married to Edel Tobin and is a loving father to Fírinne (5), Ríain (3) and 9-month old Saorla.

He has worked in the HSE since 2004 and currently works in their former Child and Family Agency, now known as Tusla.

Raised in Liskeavy, Tuam Co. Galway by Patrick and Carmel Walsh, he has a twin sister Cathy and four younger siblings including twin sisters, Laura and Linda, sister Alma, and brother, Padraic.

He attended Milltown National School and St Jarlath's secondary school in Tuam.

A fluent German speaker, he has studied German and IT, Applied Languages, and financial accounting and payroll management. He also has a degree in Addiction Studies.

His passions include hurling and Gaelic football, music, cars, politics and family.

He was diagnosed with a rare brain tumour called Liponeurocytoma at age 23 and is currently receiving treatment for inoperable cancers on the brain and the spine.

Go to www.johnwalshheadcase.com for further details and updates.